FOLKLORE OF THE SEA

FOLKLORE OF THE SEA

MARGARET BAKER

DAVID & CHARLES
Newton Abbot   London   North-Pomfret (Vt)

British Library Cataloguing in Publication Data

Baker, Margaret, b.1928
 Folklore of the sea.
 1. Seafaring life
 I. Title
 390'.4'6238   G540

ISBN 0-7153-7568-7

© Margaret Baker 1979

All rights reserved. No part of this publication may be reproduced, stored in a retrieval system, or transmitted, in any form or by any means, electronic, mechanical, photocopying, recording or otherwise, without the prior permission of David & Charles (Publishers) Limited

Typeset by Trade Linotype Limited, Birmingham
and Printed in Great Britain
by Redwood Burn Limited, Trowbridge & Esher
for David & Charles (Publishers) Limited
Brunel House   Newton Abbot   Devon

Published in the United States of America
by David & Charles Inc
North Pomfret   Vermont 05053   USA

Contents

Acknowledgements		6
List of Illustrations		7
Introduction		9
1	The Ship: Building and Naming	13
2	The Ship: Afloat	29
3	Phantom Ships and Sailors	53
4	Talismans and Taboos	76
5	Customs: Naval and Otherwise	100
6	The Perennial Sea-Serpent	125
7	The Weather-Gods	151
8	Sea-Words: the Sailor's Language	165
References		185
Bibliography		188
Index		190

Acknowledgements

I should like to thank the many people who have kindly provided information and photographs for this book, in particular:
Commander M. A. C. Moore, RN, Commanding Officer, and LREM G. H. Ford, HMS *Tartar*; J. J. Lanzon, Malta Government Tourist Board, Valletta; The Trustees of the British Museum; Mr Steve Nicovich, Biloxi Chamber of Trade, Biloxi, Mississippi; Mr J. J. Kerr, Department of Tourism, Province of Nova Scotia; Mrs P. A. Corby-Jones, Arthur Guinness Son & Company (Park Royal) Ltd, London; Lieutenant-Colonel Paul Neville, MVO, FRAM, RM; Ms Allison Buchan, The Alexander Turnbull Library, Wellington, New Zealand; Mr I. C. MacGibbon, Research Officer, Ministry of Defence, Wellington, New Zealand; Mr Roger J. Harrison and Mrs E. H. W. Tink, Fleet Air Arm Museum, Yeovilton, Somerset; Commander Tyrone G. Martin, USN, 57th in command, USS *Constitution* (IX–21); Ms Elizabeth Wiggans, The Library, National Maritime Museum, Greenwich; The Commanding Officer, HMS *Hecate*; Mr Nigel Gibbs, Gibbs & Co (Ship Management) Ltd, Newport, Monmouthshire; the Chairman, Austin & Pickersgill Ltd, Sunderland; Commander S. G. Clark, MBE, BA, AMBIM, RN (Retd), Royal Naval Museum, Portsmouth; Mr Bill Kreh, Editor, *Navy Times*, Washington, DC; Mr W. Wilkinson, MBE, Editor, *Navy News*, Portsmouth; The Librarian, Metropolitan Borough of Wolverhampton; Duncan S. Gray of Vancouver; and finally, Mary Farnell, of Wendover, for her valuable assistance with photography.

List of Illustrations

Plates

Maltese fishing-boats decorated with *oculi* (*Photo* Malta Government Tourist Board)	16
The figurehead from the training-ship *Eurydice*, lost near Portsmouth in 1878 (*Photo* Portsmouth Royal Naval Museum)	21
Launching the *Strathdirk* at Sunderland (*Photo* Austin & Pickersgill Ltd)	31
Bluenose's likeness on Canada's ten-cent piece	34
Bluenose II, replica of the famous Nova Scotian fishing-schooner (*Photo* Nova Scotia Travel Bureau)	35
The ship's bell of HMS *Colossus* (*Photo* Fleet Air Arm Museum, Yeovilton)	37
The *Great Eastern* in a storm (Nineteenth-century print)	49
The 'Great Storm' of 1703 – a scene in the Downs anchorage (Nineteenth-century print)	62
COEMN 'Phil' Filby, of the Royal Navy and HMS *Tartar*, puts a model ship into a bottle (*Photo* LREM G. H. Ford, HMS *Tartar*)	83
Fred Wunpound, last ship's cat in the Royal Navy (*Photo* Navy News: HMS *Hecate*)	85
Peggy, bulldog mascot of HMS *Iron Duke* (*Author's collection*)	86
'Blessing the Fleet' at Biloxi, Mississippi (*Photo* Biloxi Chamber of Commerce)	98
'Crossing the Line' on HMS *Hood*, 1923 (*Author's collection*)	111
The sea-serpent seen by HMS *Daedalus* in 1848 (*Photo* Illustrated London News)	131
Odysseus and his crew pass the Sirens (*Photo* Trustees of the British Museum)	137

Figures

1	A medieval sea-monster	126
2	Octopus, 'devil-fish' or 'kraken'	127
3	A 'sea-monk' and a 'sea-bishop'	139
4	Seals were mistaken for mermaids	141
5	Flying-fish	146
6	The John Dory with St Peter's marks	147
7	Perhaps an old sailor?	148
8	Poseidon or Neptunus Rex, King of the Ocean	157
9	Stormy petrel, harbinger of rough weather	161

Introduction

The past hundred years have seen vast changes at sea. Today's sophisticated mariners ignore or smile at sea superstitions and customs; many are forgotten, and maritime folklore is a shadow of its former self. And yet some beliefs and ways, old as the ship herself, stubbornly refuse to depart or diminish. A lively example is the enduring dislike of leaving port on a Friday which, it is said, has caused Britain's National Union of Seamen to seek the shipowners' assurance that no vessel will ever be scheduled to sail on Friday the thirteenth.

In 1934 Captain George Whitfield of Union-Castle looked back on *Fifty Thrilling Years at Sea* and remembered the sailing shellback of half a century earlier. None was more ignorantly superstitious than he who believed in ocean spectres, the 'wave-demon' – a green-faced ghoul – the 'trough-master' of storms and the 'wind-devil'. 'Some flouted them, of course, but they were never altogether decried.' Such spectres meant death; watchkeepers had gone mad when they spied the 'corposant' slithering on the yardarm. Whistling raised a gale; glimpses of derelicts on moonlit nights made sea-phantoms; sea-serpents and mermaids were never impossible. Building and launching rituals were as vital to a ship's safety as the state of her hull; her name no less. These were the dicta of the sea.

In the heyday of the sailing-ship there had been a thousand charms: a shark's tail nailed aloft won the wind-god's favour; a pocketed caul saved a man from drowning; a gold coin in the mast-step solicited Fortuna's smile. Intrinsically valueless as such practices were, they valuably reinforced the sailor's own confidence, his will to win through in situations such as Samuel Kelly, an eighteenth-century seaman, described: 'No sooner is one peril over but another comes rolling on, like the waves of a full-grown sea . . .' They enjoyed a full life, and it is not quite over. The *Sir Winston Churchill* sail-training schooner, launched in 1966, carries Churchill crowns under her masts. German U-boats on South Atlantic patrol in World War II were seen to be wearing porpoise tails (more easily obtained than sharks'), but the intention was now blurred – wind was no longer required, the tails merely brought good luck.

To old sailors the sea was double-faced, almost capable of thought and action; on the one hand the sparkling sun-kissed provider of livelihoods, on the other the white-lashed 'widow-maker', ready to call the sailor to another world. He was exposed to all her moods with little but seamanship to protect him. At sea the gods' anger spoke loud and it must be appeased with proper rituals. Only when steamships and radio made voyages shorter and safer did superstition, a natural response to danger, decline, its work done.

Change at sea came from several directions. In the nineteenth century the great swing from sail to steam saw the beginning of the end for the brilliant, capricious, wooden sailing-ship. In Britain 1870 was a watershed; in that year registered sailing tonnage reached $4\frac{1}{2}$ million tons, that of steamers 901,000 tons. But from that year sailing tonnage steadily declined, while steamer tonnage increased. Animism was to be poorly served by engines and iron hulls. The editor of *Woodenboat* makes the same point for an even newer boat-building material: 'I don't know anybody who says of a glass-fibre boat, "I feel the soul of this boat" . . . A lot of people feel that their wooden boats are alive.' By the century's end better education and improved pay and living conditions were bringing a less credulous man to sea. The old loneliness when a sailing-ship beat for weeks across the great Southern Ocean, domain of the albatross, meeting no one, was over. Shorter passages killed customs such as 'Saturday night at sea' and 'dead horse'.

With steam and mechanisation heavy shipwork ended; chanties lost their purpose and were heard no more at sea, except on training-ships and perhaps on the few remaining windships afloat until World War II, and today in those of the West Indies. By the 1920s the practical chanty had essentially vanished, but by then it was a song-form increasingly popular with choirs and singers, and in this way at least, the chanty has survived. The year 1869 marked the end of the greatest days of the sailing-ship and the Panama Canal in 1914 killed the last sailing route round Cape Horn. Bred-in-the-bone seamen had become noticeably rarer long before that. The following stimulating dialogue, overheard when an American sailing battleship paid off in 1843, exactly captures the old relationship between the shellback and the sea, an atmosphere conducive to superstition and tradition, and one which is quite dead today:

'Sink the sea!' cried the forecastleman. 'Once more ashore and you'll never catch old Boom Bolt afloat, I mean to settle down in a sail loft. Shipmates, take me by the arms and swab up the lee scuppers with me, but I mean to steer a clam cart before I go again to a ship's wheel. Let the Navy go by the board, to sea agin, I won't.'

'Start my soul-bolts, maties, if any more blue peters and sailing signals fly at my fore!' cried the captain of the head. 'My wages will buy a wheelbarrow if nothing more.'

'I have taken my last dose of sails,' cried the captain of the waist. ' "Blast the sea, shipmates," say I.'

Within a week all three had signed on again.

Two world wars added to influences for change. More customs succumbed to economic necessity. It is difficult to imagine many shipping companies today painting a narrow blue 'mourning line' round the hulls of their vessels to signify the death of a prominent member of their firm, yet the practice was known until 1939 and even later. Navies too were changing: 'big ships' were disappearing; after 1945 submarines became capital ships and such ceremonies as 'Rolling Home' came to an end.

Yet despite these changes 'luck' is still a word never far from the lips of those who must confront the ocean at her grimmest. After the difficult transfer of a casualty from a tanker in the English Channel in 1974, Coxswain Ben Tart of the Dungeness lifeboat said, '. . . it's not only judgement, you've got to have some *luck*'. And when luck is needed some of the old supplicatory rituals tend to be recalled (amulets are never more popular than in wartime). Sea-magic survives vigorously today in the world's fishing fleets – with small vulnerable boats still dependent upon weather, nature and chance.

Sea-lore is a vast subject and inevitably this book must be a personal selection only. 'Different ships, different long splices' is a sound axiom: there are numberless embellishments to such favourites as the 'Flying Dutchman'. Bright embroidery marks the genre, the raconteurs and historians rarely agree on details. To label beliefs and customs 'obsolete' merely invites proof of their survival; they may be more robust than first glance suggests. Traditionalists, often on sail-training vessels, eagerly preserve old ways and words; nautical museums grow in popularity; many believe that the ship's ethos as much as the ship herself should be preserved. Navies, always great tradition-bearers, appreciate its importance in recruiting and fighting; and if battle-cruisers no longer fly paying-off pendants, submarines certainly do. Fishing fleets are still blessed at the season's start; lucky ships receive silver bells; and supertankers are launched with clear courtesies to the old gods. Perhaps after all, at sea as elsewhere, '*plus ça change, plus c'est la même chose*' is as good a motto as any.

1 The Ship: Building and Naming

Traces remain of protective arcana once called into play by ship-builders to protect the vessels they built. Until well into the nineteenth century the most sceptical of owners appreciated the wider value of publicly observing such precautions – they might be instrumental in attracting a good crew (in the gossiping world of the port the news soon went round) and therefore safety for the ship and profits for the owner. Sailors' endorsement of occult preparations taken at the outset added promise to a ship's career. Unless untypically free from superstition, competent seamen who had choice naturally avoided 'unlucky', ill-prepared ships. Even in the unemotional world of modern shipping, 'lucky' and 'unlucky' reputations are quickly made and stick like glue, sometimes for a ship's lifetime.

The Heart of the Ship

Laying the keel, the lowest longitudinal timber or line of metal plates from which the ship will rise, and therefore the 'heart of the ship', is an occasion for ceremony. In Brittany *on arrose le bateau* and, until the new ship's health has been drunk, no building can begin. Some knock the first nail into place through a horseshoe for luck. In 1921, obedient to another tradition, the Duke of Devonshire, Governor-General of Canada, hammered a red-beribboned gilded spike into the keel beam to start the work on the champion Nova Scotian fishing-schooner *Bluenose*; in 1963 the same custom attended the birth of her replica, *Bluenose II*. Deriving from this custom is the jovial order to novitiates in the United States Navy to go below 'to polish the golden rivet' – imaginary and in the darkest corner. As the witch-deterrent colour of blood and life, red is a proper choice for decorations to save the vessel from those with the menacing attribute of the 'evil-eye'. It is sad to report that after a long history the US Navy in 1977 abandoned as 'expensive and time-consuming' most ceremonies of keel-laying which had grown from the old legal requirement that keels be 'authenticated well and truly laid'.

A westerly wind and a making tide, the swooping professional support of gulls (old sailors reincarnated), a glowing moon and sunshine to ensure, by imitative magic, abundant cargoes, bumper catches and water ever under the keel, were hoped-for omens at this moment. Less happily, if the first shaping blow struck fire the ship would eventually burn, and if blood accidentally flowed during her building she would be a 'death-ship'. Never noticeably restrained in language, shipwrights did not swear in the presence of the semi-sacred keel or nothing would go right. To change a ship's design after building had begun brought only ill-luck. The taboos of the sea – hares, pigs, priests and women, especially red-haired virgins, with malign influences – were banned from shipyards. Inauspicious for keel-laying were Thursday, day of Thor, god of thunder and storm, and Friday, attainted long before the Crucifixion confirmed its ill-reputation, a day named for the Old Norse goddess Frigg, Odin's wife, beautiful and dangerous, no sailor's ideal.

As late as the nineteenth century, bones were concealed in house walls and floors as token 'foundation sacrifices'. Much earlier the Vikings, masters of ship-magic, had laid their longships with a living sacrifice, that they might sail straight and true. In time bones replaced victims. Shoes or shoe-shapes were also used as good-luck charms. Investigated in 1969, the Dutch East Indiaman *Amsterdam*, wrecked near Hastings, Sussex, on her maiden voyage in 1748, provided the improbable finds, deep in the orlop deck, of a horse skull and a shoe-last, about whose protective function there could be little doubt. In some communities the discreet insertion of 'lucky' woods such as ash, rowan, or dogwood, abhorred by witches, is proper in keel-building. No boat left the Gabarus, Nova Scotia, boatyards without dogwood tholepins; chestnut made a boat faster; black walnut, despite its excellence, ' draws lightning' and is still avoided by American boatyards. To appease the jealous ocean-gods a Scottish master boat-builder in person thrust a gold coin into the keel-splicing, its place a secret except to the depositor and the ship's owner – in all effective magic, secrecy is essential. Here was an antique practice for, during excavations for London's County Hall in 1910, two coins were discovered in the ribs of a Roman ship sunk deep in South Bank mud; and, carefully wrapped in canvas, a gold coin dated 1618 lay in the keel of a Spaniard found in the Orkneys in 1810.

Favoured boat-builders lengthily monitored by canny customers never lacked trade. In the Mull of Kintyre the Mackenzie yard was famous: had not an earlier Mackenzie gallantly assisted a stranded mermaid back to the sea and in return been granted his dearest wish – that he might build unsinkable boats from which no man would ever be lost?

'Oculi' and Figureheads

As ships of substance sprang to life, carpenters and carvers contrived their decorations, worn in varying forms from earliest seafaring days. On poop or afterdeck Roman ships carried altars dedicated to the vessel's guardian deity, her *tutela*. The very name 'poop' is said to derive from *puppis*, the

Latin name for the stern deck where the deities were set up; the respect still accorded a warship's quarterdeck perhaps springs from the genuflections offered to their shrines. A carving of AD 200 in the Torlonia Museum, Rome, portrays the captain of a merchantman sprinkling incense upon a blazing altar fire as his ship enters Rome harbour, with a thanksgiving ceremony in progress about a Victory, the *tutela*.

'My guardian deity is yellow-haired Minerva – and may she be such, I pray!' – cried Ovid in *Tristia*, 'and my ship takes its name from a painted helmet [a helmeted bust of the goddess] on the bow.' The bold ship-distinguishing *episemon, parasemon* or 'name-device' was valuable identification in an age lacking telescopes. Greek galleys favoured a *stylis* or pole-device. (Of the same family were the sheet-iron 'caps of liberty' worn at the mastheads of French men-of-war during the Revolution, and the metal 'sark' sported by *Cutty Sark* in port to mark her from racing rivals.) Whole Greek squadrons might wear the same device, like the gilded nereids which marked Achilles' squadron at Troy.

Maltese fishing-boats with on their bows the 'eye of Horus' whose stare protects boats against the 'evil-eye'

Widely found is the 'all-seeing eye of the ancients', beloved by Greek, Roman, Egyptian, Carthaginian, Phoenician, Arab, Portuguese and Eastern seafarers, the 'eye of Horus and Osiris', the *oculus*, whose bold stare deflected hostile magic, intimidated human foes and, with luck, halted the very sea-gods themselves. Nothing subdued the evil-eye more effectively than a dose of its own glaring medicine. The Chinese believed too, that 'eyeless' a ship was blind, unable to look out for herself; as a ships' chandler curtly advised a passenger enquiring about the 'great goggle eyes' on a vermilion-painted junk: 'No hab eyes, how can see?' Later the part of the ship 'right up front' where a lookout is stationed in fog, became known as 'the eyes of the ship'.

At Red Stone Cove, Massachusetts, about 1879 Samuel Drake came upon:

> ... stranded and broken in two, a long-boat, brought years ago from China, perhaps on the deck of some Indiaman. Its build was outlandish, so unlike the wherries that were by, yet so like the craft that swim in the turbid Yang Tse. I took a seat in it, and was carried to the land of pagodas, opium and mandarins. Its sheathing was of camphor wood which still exhaled the pungent odor of the aromatic tree. On either quarter was painted an enormous eye that seemed to follow you about the strand.[1]

Oculi retain a place at sea. The Solomon Islanders fix a 'protective spirit' with huge mother-of-pearl eyes to their canoes; the white, rose and blue crescent-shaped sardine-boats round Caparica, Furadouro and Esphinho in Portugal are dressed with eyes against the *mau olhado* – evil-eye. Maltese fishing-boats, blue, green and red, with gold rubbing-strakes, carry painted eyes with eyebrows and, while the custom is beginning to die, older fishermen still feel happier with *oculi* in place. Even a complete product of the technological age, the 17,000-ton freighter *Mormacsun*, entered the sea at Oakland, California, in 1940 with eyes upon her bow for luck.

From such beginnings grew the robust figureheads and carvings of later years. Several superstitions underlie the use of figureheads; the animistic vision of the ship as a living entity, naturally needing a 'head'; the need to propitiate and subdue the sea- and weather-gods; the ship's need to see her own way across the ocean. Figureheads, in some form, were used from ancient times: the Ancient Egyptians protected their ships with holy birds; the Phoenicians favoured swift horses; the Greeks a boar's head, symbolising aggression. In northern waters the serpent's head of the longships was much seen (as well as the forked 'tails'). Motifs were to prove long-lasting; a third-century Roman galley's owner decorated her with a goose-necked sternpost in stripes of brown and white, with, on the stern, a scarlet *oculus* and a sky-blue sea-monster; much later the clipper *Sea Serpent*, built at Portsmouth, New Hampshire, in 1850, carried a full-length image of the 'Great American Sea-Serpent', whose appearances had electrified New England coasts thirty years before.

Early figureheads were mounted on the beakhead. Changes in ship design in the sixteenth century opened the way for figureheads mounted under the bowsprit, in the manner familiar today. At first animal heads predominated on warships and on such as East Indiamen; top favourite in many countries was the lion's head, although dragons, unicorns and other beasts were seen and, on important ships, figureheads such as that of the *Sovereign of the Seas* – 'King Edgar trampling on seven kings'. This magnificent ship, built for Charles I of England in 1637, loaded with carving, reached the pinnacle of allegorical extravagance. The Dutch nicknamed her the 'Golden Devil'. Less spectacular perhaps, but no less vivid and skilful, were the carvings – mermaids, dolphins, flowers, classical motifs – which decorated stern and trail boards, bollards and catheads, from the fourteenth to the nineteenth century.

In the second half of the eighteenth century figureheads expressing the ship's name and character came into fashion. The great Spanish *Santissima Trinidad* carried a group representing the Holy Trinity. Figureheads became works of art

THE SHIP: BUILDING AND NAMING

created by the most gifted carvers of their day, finding fullest expression in portraiture of primitive charm and colour, or in purest white, with *oculi* brought up to date in the figureheads' glaring, thyroidal eyes. Artists' hands expertly achieved curves of flesh and drifts of fabric; and apparent forward movement, as though urging the ship to greater speeds, was part of figurehead magic.

Captains hated losing a figurehead through storm or accident. When one was carried away in high seas, a shipwright suggested a substitute he had seen lying unused in the yard, but the affronted master cried out: 'Do I seem one who would pick up with another's cast-off figurehead? I'd sooner think of taking up with a new *wife!*' Sailors' yarns told of Pacific Islanders worshipping figureheads washed up on remote beaches; even chips from these powerful amulets were prized – whittling by departing sailors of an old figurehead set up on Custom House or 'Wooden Dolly' Quay, North Shields, in 1814, was so persistent that to date five replacements, the latest set in position in 1958, have been called for.

Superstition governed other ship decorations. In New York in 1851, a little wooden sailor, in sennit hat and bellbottoms, holding on his knee the ship's binnacle, was carved for the *N.B. Palmer*, but although acclaimed as charming and much admired by the crew, the figure made only one run to China. Wheelsmen complained that its eyes moved at night and distracted them from the compass.[2]

A figurehead, with rouged cheeks and sparkling eyes, personification of the ship's spirit, was never desecrated. In the St Lawrence River in 1920, when a careless towline severed the arm of the figurehead of the *Grand Duchess* ex *Hesperus*, survivor of the great iron clipper fleet on the Australia run, old hands were quick to attribute later setbacks to 'losin' der arm'. The only remedy in such a case was to restore the ship's psychic wholeness with immediate replacement. When the wooden hat of the Duke of Brunswick, figurehead of HMS *Brunswick*, was shot away during a tussle with the *Vengeur* on the 'Glorious first of June' Captain Harvey, aware of his crew's distress at this mutilation, at once handed the ship's carpenter his own cocked hat to be hammered into place on the duke's bald pate.

Figureheads often reflected a ship's occupation. Naval heroes, warriors, statesmen and rulers were proper to warships. In 1834 the USS *Constitution* received her third figurehead, generally regarded as the finest of the American naval group, the cloaked President Andrew Jackson, with hat, stick and scroll (the constitution). It was carved by Laban S. Beecher of Boston, an acknowledged master. George III, caparisoned as a Roman emperor, sword at side, red cloak at shoulder, supported by Fame and Fortune, led the *Royal Sovereign* to Trafalgar. Merchantmen enhanced their trading images with the sedate and respectable, whalers favoured the homely . . . a life-sized *Alice Knowles* of New Bedford, in high button boots and country day dress, sturdy, domestic, redolent of apple pie and warm kitchens, was, her crew declared, a better reminder of home than a portrait. The relationship might even be emotional: on the *Princess* the only confidante for a thousand miles was consulted by a lovesick crew whose captain saw them creeping forrard after dark to pour their troubles into sympathetic wooden ears.

With the coming of the clippers the final and most romantic period opened for the figurehead. Female figures outnumbered male and they were often bare-breasted, for it is an ancient nautical belief that a storm will quieten if a woman exposes herself to it *nuda corpore*. Figureheads were by way of permanent insurance. The figureheads of the 'greyhounds of the seas' were haunting in their suggestion of fragrant cargoes and ships going like swallows: 'Mandarin, in a pleated blue robe . . . with a red hat, and a yellow tassel, and holding a small scroll . . .' ran the *Kaisow*'s specification. The carver of a 'dragon' for the *Yang-tsze* received £13 10s from a total building bill of £14,724 5s. Princesses, Indian maidens, chieftains, figures of legend, literature and stage leaned glamorously into the weather, buoyantly extending the ship's lines. Captains' and owners' daughters were honoured to be asked to act as models; the *Belle of Bath* (Maine) carried an

The figurehead from the training-ship *Eurydice* which sank near Portsmouth in 1878 with the loss of 194 officers and men, after capsizing in a freak squall. The staring eyes common in figureheads derived from earlier *oculi*, and bared breasts were said to quieten **storms**

$8\frac{1}{2}$ft-tall figurehead in a gold and white balldress of 1877. It was a portrait of the captain's daughter and the carver, another master, Charles A. L. Sampson of Bath.

The *Cutty Sark*, most famous of clippers, now in permanent dry-dock at Greenwich, has a bare-breasted Nannie, the witch of Robert Burns' poem, reaching out in pursuit of Tam o' Shanter's mare Meg, as he spurs for the Brig o' Doon. Nannie's short chemise named the ship:

> Her cutty sark, o' Paisley harn,
> That while a lassie she had worn,
> In longitude tho' sorely scanty,
> It was her best, and she was vauntie.

In *Cutty*'s racing days, after a passage when she had indeed 'gone like a witch', apprentices pushed a 'tail' of teased rope-yarns into Nannie's hand. Every sailor who served in the *Cutty Sark* spoke of her with affection; her figurehead, carved by F. Hellyer, a famous craftsman of Blackwall, was part of her enduring mystique.

The captain of the barque *Clan McLeod* (later the *James Craig*) cherished a figurehead of a stately Highland chieftain in gay bonnet and plaid. Only on Sunday mornings in port did an apprentice reverently lift its canvas cover (worn at sea 'to keep the McLeod warm') as the captain raised his hat, with the courtly greeting 'Guid moornin', McLeod!' When an irreverent joker tied a whisky bottle to the McLeod's sporran and supplied him with an oakum beard and clay pipe, the captain's fury, his raving in Gaelic, his verbal fireworks, which lasted for over a week, were never forgotten.

With the coming of steam, and with iron ships, the popularity of figureheads began to decline (although in a minor revival the Fred Olsen Line is again using them). A wooden figure did not chime with an iron ship; bowsprits disappeared, attachment was difficult; the magical wooing of weather and sea mattered less and less. But rejection nevertheless came slowly. *Warrior*, the first British ironclad, had a figurehead; the steam sloop HMS *Cadmus*, launched in 1903, is reputed to have been the last Royal Navy ship to carry one. A latecomer in the North Atlantic trade was the crowned eagle of the German liner *Imperator*. But the eagle, soon damaged in a storm, was quietly removed and never replaced. As far as could be told no one regretted its passing, yet when the Allies appropriated the ship as part of World War I reparations the *Imperator*'s former crew wasted no time in roundly blaming this humiliation upon the loss of the eagle, years before.

In navies, figurehead magic was naturally re-invested in ships' badges or crests, often heraldic or fusing name and associations. The US nuclear submarine *Seadragon* displayed a red, green and orange dragon, breathing fire, coiling up angrily, atom in claw, with the Chinese motto 'From the depths I rule!' And for her badge HMS *Sterling* chose a golden sovereign and the happy motto 'Good as Gold'.

'Spankin' Sassy Names'

Improved sea-safety has made aural reassurance in ship-names less pressing; naming has lost its former significance and too much should not be read into twentieth-century names. But a hint of former magic lingers and still helps to mould a vessel's luck. Name-magic once carried much weight. In 1842 at Kennebunkport, Maine, at the launching of the *Isadore*, named for her builder's daughter, an old man grumbled, 'I've seed them barkeys as could almost ship a crew for nothin' they carried such spankin' sassy names! We'd have rather an out-and-out *Yankee* name any day of the week!' He spoke of immemorial fears of the unusual, only too likely to attract hostile spirits to work woe; and his doubts were soon confirmed for the outlandishly-named and therefore unlucky *Isadore* was wrecked on the dangerous Isle of Shoals on her maiden voyage.

Ill-starred, infective connotations are taboo in ship-naming; battle defeats and disasters (never another *Titanic*) are forgotten; but the victorious, the record-breakers, the 'lucky' ships are reborn repeatedly and illustrious forebears pass their good fortune on. In 1807 at Yarmouth, Nova Scotia, three schooners, *Victory, Lord Nelson* and *Trafalgar* – among the thousands which would bear names born of that incomparable year, 1805 – took the water. And in 1856 approving glances greeted the début of the *Glad Tidings*, which sailed with the inestimable advantage of one Horatio Nelson, master.

The plain commercial sea-world of today pays little attention to ship-naming, yet certain old rules seem to wear well. Expediency may force many mutations but small owners, at least, dislike the necessity. Nautical legend recalls that in 1934, when the name *Queen Mary* was selected for the new Cunarder, only after much coaxing was the owner of a much smaller *Queen Mary*, already afloat, persuaded that to consider his ship *Queen Mary II* would not injure her. Changing a name, a delicate business, is positively disliked in Ireland and the United States, where 'it means a death'. Usually, observed Captain Sir David Bone, Commodore Master of the Anchor Line, in *Landfall at Sunset* (1955), sailors prefer not to tinker but, if unavoidable, name-changing is discreet and generally devoid of ceremonies of adult baptism. Sometimes mandatory changes follow transfers to other flags or fleets (which may favour a series, like Blue Star's *Tuscan Star*, *Trojan Star*, *Californian Star*) or changes may be intended to obscure – even to conceal – a ship's identity. Misdeeds, cargo troubles or ill-luck with captains make her disliked by underwriters, shippers and pilots. She is sold. New owners begin again and after a brief announcement the new name is quietly painted on.

But can the Ethiopian always change her skin? The London *Telegraph*, February 1885, thought not:

> The steamer with the pretty name of *Ianthe*, was the *Rose*, and before she was the *Rose* she was that most ill-fated ship which, if 'not built in the eclipse', was certainly attended with 'curses dark', the *Daphne*, whose launch on the Clyde, it will be recollected, caused the drowning of an appalling number of men. She sank in the Clyde as the *Daphne*; she

was raised, and then sank in Portrush harbour as the *Rose*; she was raised again, and, still as the *Rose*, she ran ashore on Big Cumbrae. Then she was got off and lost sight of for a little, and now reappears as the *Ianthe*, comfortably lodged on the mud which she seems to love so well, and to which her instincts regularly direct her, after having threatened to go down in deep water, and then changing her mind and plumping on a rock. She is evidently an unlucky ship . . .

In the United States, Britain and Germany, ships are firmly feminine, but not so in France. When the *Normandie* was named, the influential French Academy favoured *La Normandie*. One might properly speak of *le paquebot Normandie* but never *Le Normandie*! But at Penhoët the conservative shipyard workers disagreed. Ships were masculine, they insisted. Finally the namers settled for *Normandie sans l'article*. A similar row broke out in Germany when the problem of *Die* or *Das Vaterland* was confronted. Generally though the feminine nature of ships has long been accepted: Sir Alec Rose's *Lively Lady*, heroine of circumnavigation, is of an antique line. Behind some names must surely lie episodes when the contrariness of ships and sweethearts seemed at one. In Yarmouth in 1815, the *Pam-be-Civil* splashed into the sea; in St John in 1855 the *Go Ask Her!*; and in 1867 in Prince Edward Island, a disillusioned owner, reflecting no doubt on sad experience, sent the *Great Deceiver* on her way.

Despite bold entries in the registries from the 1850s onwards of such dashing names as *Hurricane* and *Black Squall* ('thousand-ton audacity', said old sailors), many felt that the sea's nature precluded boasting. No sailor could afford to take the chance of offending. For so frail a creation as a ship, arrogant names of tempests and wild winds, grand to the ear, might provoke the rival *genius mari.* 'There shall not two Atlantics be . . .' declared a contemporary heavily when the White Star's *Atlantic* sank off Nova Scotia in 1873. His audience fully took his point. The thoughtful were wont to consider the flamboyant *Queen of the Seas* (foundered

Formosa Channel, 1860, with all hands); *Empress of the Seas* (burned, 1861); *Queen of the East* (lost in the Pacific, 1872); *The Queen of the Pacific* (lost north of Pernambuco, 1859); *Champion of the Seas* (abandoned off the Horn, 1876). There were many others. 'Self-fulfilling in disaster; thus are the high brought low,' wrote one sententious mariner.

Safer by far were names civilly inviting the goodwill of the King of the Ocean. For the clipper *Neptune's Car* the choice proved triumphantly correct. On passage to San Francisco in 1856, her first officer was under arrest when, several thousand miles from port, the captain was struck blind and deaf with 'brain-fever'. Yet undismayed Mrs Patten, the captain's wife, aged only nineteen, with, said the crew dotingly, the aid of Old Neptune himself, solicitous for a namesake, brought the ship safely in and richly deserved the toasts of the waterfront. The charm of this age-old magic was also felt by Sir Alec Rose when he named his first boat *Neptune's Daughter* because he felt the sea – Father Neptune – to be alive, worthy of his respect and perhaps disposed to deal kindly with a vessel so-named.[3]

Warships' names impress with pugnacity or imply alliances with powerful gods (three *Neptunes*, French, Spanish and British, fought at Trafalgar). The United States Navy carried such bonny fighting names as *Pocahontas* and *Mohican* but, wrote Captain A. T. Mahan, USN, the naval historian, by 1907 the once-abundant Indian names had vanished – or worse been relegated to *tugboats*. ('Since they with their names have passed into the world of ghosts – can there be for them a sea in the happy hunting ground?') Today the Indian link is upheld by Canadian warships alone: US ships generally bear names of states, cities, battles or naval heroes. In 1976 at Bath, Maine, was launched the fifth *Oliver Hazard Perry*, named after the officer who engaged the British fleet in Lake Erie in 1813. Her launching was appropriately sponsored by Mrs Morgan Hebard, Perry's great-great-great-granddaughter. The Royal Navy regularly brings forward famous old names for its latest ships. In 1976 for example was commissioned the nuclear-powered Fleet hunter-attack submarine, HMS *Superb*, ninth of her name: the first had been the French prize *Superbe*, entered in 1710 under her English name.

Fish and sea-animals provide names for submarines, as though association with marine residents enhances underwater prowess. Until motorised days, owners of fishing vessels, avoiding brashness and mindful of the Breton prayer, 'O God, be good to me, Thy sea is so wide and my ship is so small...' chose names humble and pious, most unlikely to enrage vengeful spirits: *Girl Pamela, Auntie Gus, Our Bairns, Ave Maria* and *Dieudonné*. Reliable trading often distinguishes merchantmen, with such blameless names as *Voyager, Harvester, Express* and *Merchant*. With cruise-ships was born the latest tradition, one of sun, fun and dream-worlds, reflected in such names as Cunard's *Countess* and P & O's *Sun Princess*.

Sailors collectively borrow their ship's name. At Port Mahon, Minorca, once the base of the US Mediterranean Squadron, a tombstone to Alexander Graves, 'Quarter Gunner of the US frigate *Brandywine*', illustrated the convention:

> Faithful in duty; contented in his mind,
> And died lamented by the *Brandywines*.

Tradition-cherishing admirals enjoyed addressing captains by the names of their commands. Thus, as late as 1930, Captain Max Horton, RN, to be Commander-in-Chief, Western Approaches, during the grimmest period of the Battle of the Atlantic, was ringingly and appropriately addressed in correspondence by Admiral W. W. Fisher as 'My Dear *Resolution*...'[4]

The giving of nicknames is also traditional. USS *St Louis*, 'the ship that couldn't be sunk', the only major warship to gain the open sea during the Japanese attack on Pearl Harbor in 1941, became 'Lucky Lou'; when the guns of HMS *Guerrière* failed to pierce the sides of USS *Constitution* in 1812 she became – for all time – 'Old Ironsides'. Affectionate Nelsonian tars coined 'Wheel 'em Along' for the captured *Ville de Milan*, round whose French name they refused to roll their tongues; 'Bully Ruffian' for the old warhorse *Bellerophon*; 'Polly Infamous' for *Polyphemus* and 'Eggs and Bacon' for *Agamemnon*. The nickname tradition figures in signal lore. When HMS *Penelope*, known as 'Pennyloap' (as well as 'Pepperpot'), met HMS *Antelope* at sea the latter was pleased to signal: 'At long last. Antellopee meets Pennyloap!'

Many names mentioned here – and certainly the principles underlying their selection – subscribe to an ethos which would be perfectly comprehensible to shipowners of the ancient world. In two millennia tastes have scarcely changed. Among the 'little ships' at Dunkirk were *Hebe, Zeus* and *Amazone*, the *Fair Breeze, Good Luck, Triton, Fortune* and *Dolphin*, direct descendants of classical favourites. For the Ancient Greeks the lesser deities were a rich repository: *Phoibe* – bright; *Charis* – grace; *Hebe* – youth; *Amphitrite* – Poseidon's consort. Names willed a ship to do her best and spoke encouragingly of her capacity to succeed; *Nike* – victory (the Royal Navy was following a venerable tradition); *Kratousa* – conquering; *Eukleia* – fame; *Eutyches* – lucky; *Euploia* – bon voyage; *Aura* – fair wind; *Boetheia* – aid; *Petomene* – flying. Appearances were foremost in the Roman *Juventus* – youth; *Pinnata* – winged. And animals, swift and predatory, magically conveyed their attributes: *Lupa* – she-wolf; *Crocodilus* and *Draco* – paralleled today by *Lynx, Tiger* and *Bulldog*.

The Roman navy favoured mythological and river names with *Apollo, Juno, Triton, Danae, Hercules, Vesta, Nilus* and *Tigris*. About eighty names of Roman merchantmen are recorded upon tombstones, many applauding the blessings and boons of Roman rule – *Libertas, Pax, Concordia* and *Constantia*. Classical mariners were as anxious as any modern owner to invest their ships with good fortune. Names such as the Greek *Tyche* – 'Lady Luck' – and the Roman *Fortuna Redux* – 'good luck that brings you home', the sailor's 'Happy Returns' – carried the eternal message of the sea, a message whose unchanging nature can be confirmed by a visit to any harbour today.[5]

2 The Ship: Afloat

The ship awaits naming and launching and little is left to chance lest accident or neglect create a 'jinx' of life-long stain. Launching beliefs are frailer than they were; once Wednesday was 'best day of all for the job', and Friday shunned, but in cheerful rebellion Cunard launched the *Countess* at San Juan on Friday, 13 August 1976, a choice of date which a hundred years earlier would have limited her charms for susceptible passengers.

As with a bride, a ship bathed in sunshine will be happy. 'The sun always shines on *Nautilus*,' said the crew of the first nuclear submarine to pass beneath the North Pole, a saying which originated on launching day when a thick fog overhung the Thames River at Groton, Connecticut. At the last moment, just as Mrs Dwight Eisenhower was about to swing the champagne, the fog burned away, so dramatically that many spoke of a minor miracle.[6] Tide permitting, a forenoon launching – sun ascendant – endows the newcomer with rising fortunes, if a warship with satisfying knocks at the enemy. So favourable are attendant gulls and porpoises that many toss chopped fish 'chum' into the water to ensure their attendance.

Hesitation symbolises setbacks in the vessel's career: no lucky ship ever stuck on the ways, which are well lubricated beforehand – for practical reasons admittedly, but sympathetic magic is also served. (The *Queen Mary* slipped away over 150 tons of tallow and 50 tons of soft soap.) If wooden ways catch fire as the ship creaks over them she will be 'lively as the leaping flame'. For luck the tugs which swing her round follow the 'sunwise turn', the luck-bringing arc of life.

The touch of the sponsor, in England and America almost always feminine, endows the ship with luck. A bottle of wine was once flung free-style at the bow by the sponsor, with a lively chance of error or accident. Today the bottle usually swings forward on a decorated cord to smash in a glitter of glass and wine. Until the seventeenth century wine was poured over the bow from a silver goblet which was then tossed to Poseidon. This expansive and expensive gesture did not last!

Modern launchings, glittering public-relations performances, derive from ancient custom. The primitive occult importance of the occasion is plain in the extraordinary fanfare afforded a new ship compared with that, say, greeting a new aircraft. Bands play, the clergy stand by with blessings, ships sound their whistles (for loud noises frighten away evil spirits) and when the ship is safely in the water a congratulatory luncheon follows. The idea is not new; when the *Beaulieu* was launched at Buckler's Hard, Hampshire, in 1791, Henry Adams, her builder, entertained eighty to a banquet, and the guests danced until three in the morning.

The Vikings believed that jealous sea-gods demanded a life for every new ship entering their element and lashed a useless prisoner to the ways so that his blood provided the mollifying offering. Until the nineteenth century, blood baptism was essential to any war-canoe's welfare in Fiji, Tonga and Tahiti, where the human rollers were lashed between convenient plantain trees. The rite was especially important for warships whose task was to kill, and which must smell blood at the first opportunity. As late as 1784 the Bey of Tripoli launched his cruisers with a slave tied to the prow.

THE SHIP: AFLOAT

Christianity substituted quieter ceremonies of baptism and blessing. In time wine replaced blood, but in reality the splash and flow of today's champagne is sacrifice in modern dress. In Aberdeen early this century sacrifice was specifically remembered by the ducking and thrashing given to the shipwrights' apprentices. Some were thrown into the waves caused by the vessel striking the water and ducked three times.

Steel bands, libations of blood, and the potent local rum, 'Jack Iron', raise and propitiate the spirits of dead and living at traditional West Indian launchings. Laden with 'jumbie' plates of delicacies for ancestors, the flower-decked vessel stands overnight before, in a neat combination of pagan and Christian rituals, she is blessed and the blood of white cocks and hens, sheep and black goats is smeared on her timbers. In Japan baskets of birds are freed from the bow as the ship slides away, symbolising the flying floating life she will enjoy.

Smash goes the decorated champagne bottle on 27 April 1976 as Mrs Betty Bennett launches the *Strathdirk* (Peninsular & Oriental Steam Navigation Company) at Austin & Pickersgill Ltd's shipyard at Sunderland. The company has been building ships since 1826

A similar pleasing moment was captured in 1885 when Mrs Henry W. B. Glover launched the USS *Chicago* by releasing doves from red, white and blue ribbons.

Champagne is the drink of celebration and the usual, if not inevitable accompaniment to a launching. During Prohibition in the United States there was recourse to ginger ale; missionary ships have been launched with milk. Queen Elizabeth II launched HMS *Invincible* in 1977 with the traditional bottle of 'native' – in this case elderberry – wine. For *The Lady Gwendolen, The Lady Grania, The Lady Patricia*, and the *Miranda Guinness*, a bulk stout carrier launched in 1976 which carries the equivalent of nearly two million pints, the brewers, Arthur Guinness, Son & Company (Park Royal) Limited, naturally used their own famous product. Thor Heyerdahl's raft *Ra* was baptised with goat's milk, Moroccan symbol of hospitality and good wishes.

Everlastingly unlucky are ships launched with water. Tradition relates that it was tried to no effect in the first attempts to launch USS *Constitution*, which apparently knew better than to compromise herself and only consented to budge when 'Commodore James Sever stood at the heel of the bowsprit and ... baptised the ship with a bottle of choice old Madeira.' But in 1858 the USS *Hartford* got away safely after a tripartite watery anointing: Commodore Downes' daughter smashed a bottle of Hartford Springs water across her bow, Commodore Streingham's daughter cracked a bottle of Connecticut River water on her figurehead and Lieutenant Preble poured seawater over her deck.

In the Middle Ages the undesired task of knocking away the blocks to free a ship for launching was assigned to criminals; later, New England shipwrights working 'under bottom' demanded – and got – copious extra grog as a reward for accepting danger. Death or injury during launching irrevocably jinxes a ship in the eyes of many sailors, prudent shipyards even enclose the champagne bottle in silver mesh to guard against flying glass. Yet if the bottle does *not* fracture, the omen is also dire and some American yards go so far as to employ an official 'jinx-buster' or 'bottle-snatcher' who stands ready to field a straying bottle and to steer it in the right direction for 'a good launch'. When at Newcastle upon Tyne in 1975 the bottle did not crack, the sponsor was quickly bundled on to a tug to chase the already-floating ship and the deed was then accomplished.

Rumbustious old-time launchings were remembered at Lunenburg, Nova Scotia, in 1963 when the *Bluenose II* was sponsored by Mrs Sidney C. Oland with, 'May God bless and protect this ship and all who sail in her. I christen thee *Bluenose II*.' Champagne splashed both ship and sponsor, always an excellent omen, and as the old order 'Wedge up!' rang out, to clanging mauls and the final keelside words 'Knock down dogs!', *Bluenose II* slipped away. To everyone's satisfaction she at once swung round, symbolically and actually confronting the open sea. Old Neptune entered another shapely vessel in his books! Fish dishes, magically appropriate to the birth of a fishing vessel, were served (200 gallons of fish chowder alone were consumed) and toasts drunk with the aid of 1,500 dozen bottles of beer piled high in 'saltbanker' dories or skiffs. It was said with pride that there were more thick heads in Lunenburg next morning than on any other day for a century.

'By custom of the yard' the champagne bottle with which Princess Alexandra launched HMS *Broadsword* in 1976 was decorated with satin ribbons and the ship's cap tally. But it had been a near thing. The ship's officers, appointed just before the launching, found to their consternation that no tallies had yet been ordered. It seemed that none would be ready for the day. But a *cri de coeur* to the tallymakers Toye, Kenning and Spencer produced sixteen tallies within forty-eight hours. It would seem that both the Royal Navy and the makers were aware of the importance of adhering to a distinctive custom. By contagious magic, to fail the first ship of a series – *Broadsword* was first of the new Type 22 frigates – might have cast a shadow not only on the ship herself but on others in the line.

In a religious ceremony so expressive of the French coasts, a new beflagged fishing-boat stood ready as the priest sprinkled her with holy water and gave the crew sacramental bread. The ship's 'godfather' and 'godmother' hammered five pins crosswise into the mast into holes stuffed with *pain bénit*. Changing little until World War II, such rituals have waned now, but many still believe that a boat 'not made Christian' will be harder to crew, and that a *patron*, unbaptised, will drown carrying his crew with him.

Bluenose's likeness on Canada's ten-cent piece

Fortuna's Tribute

The old practice of hiding coins in the mast-step for luck, before 'setting the sticks' – raising the masts – is not quite forgotten. Silver and gold coins, 'heads up', ensure fortunes to come. In 1937, in celebration of her landing the largest catch in Lunenburg's history, *Bluenose*'s likeness was put upon Canada's ten-cent pieces; these dimes were among the varied coins laid under the masts of her replica, *Bluenose II*, in 1963. Gold Churchill crowns were an obvious choice for the masts of the sail-training schooner, *Sir Winston Churchill*.

If the owner were indifferent to custom, the yardmen dipped into their own pockets, so indispensable was the ritual in readying a vessel for sea. Luxurious vessels were by no means always the best endowed: a Vanderbilt yacht, dismasted off

Bluenose II, replica of the famous fishing-schooner *Bluenose*, was launched in 1963. In the old tradition she carries coins under her masts, including the Canadian ten-cent piece portraying the original *Bluenose*, built in 1921

New England, attracted an anticipatory crowd at the dock to inspect the gold to be revealed when the mast-stump was hoisted out. They were sadly disappointed – a single cent appeared.

Was the offering a pre-paid toll to Charon, the ferryman of Hades, should the crew drown? The Portuguese still lay a coin in a coffin for this fare. A discovery in London in 1962 may throw light on the purpose: in the mast-step of a second-century AD Roman trading vessel, found in the Thames at Blackfriars, was a Domitian coin bearing the figure of Fortuna – the Roman 'Lady Luck' – in her hand a ship's rudder. It was her favour the coin sought.

The Ship's Bell

Perhaps to 'sweeten' its note (as was done with church bells) gold and silver were sometimes thrown into the casting crucible when a ship's bell was made. HMS *Malaya*'s main bell, made in 1916, contained not only gold sovereigns but silver Malay dollars. After the figurehead, no object on board attracted more occult lore than the bell and, like the figure-head, it was often preserved far beyond the life of the ship. Even if securely lashed beforehand it was said – as the ship's 'voice' – to speak for her as she was sinking. Such a disaster did not always bring silence. In a Cornish churchyard, ghostly four and eight bells proceeded from a drowned sea-captain's grave. When an unbeliever visited the grave he heard the bells and was lost on his next voyage. Drownings will follow if a glass rings with a bell-like note in a sailor's home or a naval mess. The sound must be stopped, 'then will the Devil take two soldiers instead.' Should a numerical error mar the strokes of a ship's bell, it is muffled and struck backwards to break the created ill-luck.

Sailors recognise changeling ships by bells which are rarely re-engraved after renaming. When the Royal Navy transferred the aircraft carrier *Colossus* to the French Navy in 1946 she was renamed *Arromanches*, but the French, obedient to custom,

The ship's bell of HMS *Colossus*, transferred to France in 1946 as *Arromanches*. In compliance with tradition her bell was never re-engraved, and when the ship's active life ended in 1974 the bell was returned to England for display in the Fleet Air Arm Museum, Yeovilton did not change the bell. The latter was *Colossus* to the end when, in token of association between the navies, the bell was returned to England for display at the Fleet Air Arm Museum, Yeovilton.

A ship's officer told Basil Lubbock, who gave a full account in *The China Clippers* (1914), of his delighted recognition by bell of the *Cutty Sark* at New Orleans in 1913, when she was sailing in obscurity as *Ferreira*, under the Portuguese flag. Although loved by the crew, who spoke of her affectionately as *El Pequina Camisola*, she was sadly neglected, daubed in garish colours, her brasswork, once the mate's pride and joy, caked with silver paint. With his knife the visitor carefully scraped away at her bell, now supported by a solitary dolphin, and uncovered 'Cutty Sark 1869'. 'I tapped the old bell gently with my knife and heard again the mellow sound which through the trades, the tropics and the roaring forties had for nigh half a century marked alike the dark and the sunny hours.'

The Jinxed and the Lucky

'Jinxed' vessels have reputations which persist to the breaker's yard. The fate is not uncommon. On 22 January 1969 *The Guardian* reported: 'Fire on board HMS *Blake*, one of the most jinx-ridden ships in the Royal Navy . . .' This distressful burden was borne by the huge *Great Eastern*, designed by Isambard Kingdom Brunel (1806–59) and launched on the Thames on 30 January 1858, after months of false starts. So determined was her hesitation on the ways that wags nicknamed her not Leviathan but 'Leave-her-high-and-dry-athan'. Difficult because of her innovative size (her designed tonnage was 18,914) she was a heartbreak ship, suffering from storms and mutiny, ruining owners. Her troubles were blamed on the ghosts of a riveter and his boy, accidentally sealed in the double hull, their screams muted by the racket of hammers. In August 1862, when she struck 'Great Eastern Rock' off Montauk Light, her grimly humorous officers predicted that the 'basher's' bones would shoot from the pump working on her hull; even her builder John Scott Russell thought he heard clamant tappings and imagined the ghostly basher beating on his iron cell.

This white elephant, after what can only be described as a disappointing career, was sold for breaking in 1887. When she was cut apart, wild stories, confirmed by neither police nor coroner, circulated about skeletons found, pathetic carpet-bags beside them, hammers grasped in whitened finger-bones, hammerheads worn away with knocking. Too late, said the canny, were the Jonahs brought ashore.

Clearly injured by thoughtless naming was the *Vaterland*, acquired by the United States after World War I and renamed by Mrs Woodrow Wilson, who chose *Leviathan* – 'monster of the deep'. In many ways, mostly financial, the ship foundered. Finally Captain J. M. Binks brought her back to Scotland for breaking up, later describing a voyage overhung by ruthless ill-luck. Seven fires started in the boiler room, and the boiler burst; an engineer fractured his jaw; the anchor was lost; food was so appalling that Captain Binks lived on lifeboat biscuits. Defective steering carried the ship with ghostly determination back towards New York and all night long her fog whistle blew and would not be silenced. When the ship did reach Scotland she dragged her anchors but the crew, whose articles specified pay-off 'at dusk or anchorage', struck; the ship was saved only by the last-minute exertions of a few engineers. The *Leviathan* docked on the thirteenth, just as an oil pipe burst. 'I couldn't go ahead or astern,' wrote the afflicted Binks. 'I lost the tide and had to anchor until Monday which cost another £1,000. She was a hoodoo all right.'[7]

Morning Cloud III, the yacht owned and raced by a former prime minister of Great Britain, seems to have been another, according to the superstitious. Her story is told by Edward Heath in *Sailing* (1975). At the launching of the first *Morning Cloud* the champagne bottle *twice* refused to break, but the boat's racing career was so successful that the portent was forgotten. The second *Morning Cloud*, launched without mishap, went ahead notably to win the Admiral's Cup for Britain in 1971. But with the third *Morning Cloud* trouble really came home to roost.

In the launching-day crowd on the wall overlooking the slipway stood the wife of a member of the crew; in the crush she lost her balance, fell to the concrete wall below and, suffering from severe concussion, was taken to hospital. 'This will be an unlucky boat,' Mr Heath heard someone murmur. That year the Fastnet Race was disastrous – *Morning Cloud* was constantly becalmed and for the first time the Germans won. Preparations began for the Admiral's Cup; the boat raced at Burnham but for the first time in five years no major trophy was achieved. Edward Heath had a regimental engagement in Antwerp and left the 'movement crew' to take *Morning Cloud* from Burnham, Essex, round the south-east coast of England to Cowes in the Isle of Wight. Then on 3 September the police telephoned to say that the boat had been wrecked in a furious Channel gale and that while five of the crew, two badly injured, had reached shore in a life-raft, two others had been washed overboard in the tremendous seas and were unaccounted for. On passage from Essex the weather had worsened. It had been very rough indeed going across to the North Foreland and round the Royal Sovereign light-vessel winds of 45 to 50 knots were recorded. Five or six miles from the Ower's light-vessel the boat was hit by two huge waves in succession which threw her on to her beam ends. It was at this point that the crew members were lost. With a supreme effort the survivors launched the raft and after eight wretched hours at sea were washed up on to the beach at Brighton. Significantly, in the same gale the first *Morning Cloud*, winner of the Sydney-Hobart race, and to the superstitious the progenitor of the trouble so manifest in the course of time in the third *Morning Cloud*, was torn from her moorings in Jersey and smashed to pieces against the rocks. The same sea and the same gale destroyed both.

Once sailors would show little enthusiasm for maiden voyages, regarded as little better than a shriving or cleansing of the ill-luck accumulated during building. Primitive magic ordains special precautions for 'first times' and after the maiden voyage the crew should disperse to dilute any misfortune they may have absorbed.

Sea-legend has enlarged every detail of the calamitous maiden voyage of RMS *Titanic*. Interest never wanes; new books re-examine every aspect; maritime museums report constant enquiries; and there is even talk (1978) of raising her. As recently as 1963, survivors, their descendants and devotees formed the *Titanic* Enthusiasts of America (TEA) Club which at a recent convention ate a '*Titanic* dinner', exactly reproducing the last meal on board.

The *Titanic* (46,328 tons), the largest ship in the world when she was built, left for New York on her maiden voyage on 10 April 1912 and, as might be expected, her ostentatious name and much-vaunted 'unsinkability' disturbed old sailors. As she passed hugely through Southampton Docks the *New York* and *Teutonic* both heeled dangerously at their moorings and the thoughtful asked 'What about the third time?' Their wait was short, for on the night of 14 April, off Newfoundland, the 'floating palace', moving at speed, struck an iceberg and three hours later plunged two miles to the ocean floor, in the worst peacetime accident of maritime history. Figures vary, but all agree that some 1,500 people lost their lives.

At once folklore of daunting proportions began to grow about the ship. Many recalled disturbing portents: a steward's cap badge had inexplicably fallen to pieces in his wife's hands as she stitched it on; a picture crashed from the wall of a stoker's home; the signal halyard carrying the acknowledgement of 'bon voyage' from the Old Head of Kinsale lighthouse parted; on the day before the sinking, firemen noticed a dozen rats (rare in a new ship) scurrying aft, *away* from the point where the iceberg was to strike.

Of all the outrageous fantasies which circulated, pride of place surely goes to that which blamed the calamity on an Egyptian mummy-case, later nicknamed 'The Shipwrecker'. The case, of the reign of Amenhotep IV and already held responsible for deaths among those who handled it, was presented to the British Museum by A. F. Wheeler in 1889. Thus far was hard fact: elaborate fiction was to follow. Rumour held that in 1912, following mysterious accidents to museum staff, Sir Ernest Budge (1857–1934), Keeper of Egyptian and Assyrian Antiquities, sold the case to an American collector who shipped it on the *Titanic*. Some insisted that, by some incredible chance, it had stood on the bridge when Captain Edward J. Smith gave his final orders; thus could the disaster be laid at the door of the 'Curse of the Pharoahs', vengeful towards all who desecrate their tombs. But, the story continues, the mummy-case survived; lavish bribes by a besotted owner had bought lifeboat space for it. 'The Shipwrecker' reached America to cause further destruction before its sale to a Canadian, who, understandably nervous, decided to return it to London – on the *Empress of Ireland* which, on 29 May 1914, sank in the St Lawrence river, with the loss of over 1,000 souls. This time the mummy-case sank from sight, its mischief ended at last on the river-bottom.

Sailors had long believed that ships carrying Egyptian antiquities would have difficulty reaching port. Wrote one passenger, 'The captain, seeing that we could not make way, asked if I had not got some mummy or other in my bags which hindered our progress, in which case we must return to Egypt, to carry it back.' The crew that carried 'Cleopatra's Needle' to London had no easy moment, and finished with shipwreck.

The much-relished myth of the *Titanic* is pure invention. The 'Unknown Princess from Thebes XXI Dynasty, BM Exhibit 22542' remains at the museum, it was never sold; indeed such sales are not normally permissible. This most vivid of twentieth-century folk-stories, without a grain of truth, has acquired enhanced glamour with the years.[8]

Like sailors, the public also came to believe that the *Titanic*'s overweening name contributed to her death; the events of April 1912 muted the hyperbole of liner names for many years. *Titanic* was a name best forgotten, thought the

White Star Line (perplexed by the public's refusal to do anything of the kind). When the *Carpathia* and others brought the surviving lifeboats into New York, workmen began at once to remove the doomed name. For months liners avoided the place of the sinking, swiftly designated 'haunted'; even today, nearly seventy years after the event, some shipmasters prefer to steer clear of the place where, each April, in solemn commemoration, the United States Coast Guard drops a wreath into the sea.

Captain Smith, who died with his ship, was not allowed to rest in peace. Miraculously, said some, he reached shore and was later 'seen' in a number of places. One sea-captain, an acquaintance, 'saw' Smith in a Baltimore street a week after the sinking and there were later stories of a penniless derelict, 'Whispering Smith', who died in Columbus, Ohio, and who, in a deathbed confession, insisted that he was 'Smith of the *Titanic*', concluding in obscurity his years of penance.

Among the jinxed, the British Navy recognised 'man-eaters' in the *Antiope* (the 'Antihope') and the *Achilles* which in one forty-two-month commission lost twelve sailors in falls from rigging. Some ships 'hated their crews'. The Finnish full-rigged *Grace Harwar* of the Erickson line, ungracious, accident-prone, was one who 'killed a man on every voyage' – all attributed to her first master who, when a mutinous crew threatened to accuse him of murder if he buried his wife at sea, was forced to preserve the body in the ballast. A curious presentiment of death was felt by a young sailor killed by a falling spar when on passage from Australia to England in 1929; and later his mother in Hobart declared that she, too, had known instantly of her son's death. Had not their old grandfather clock, silent for years, suddenly begun to tick? Had she not felt overpoweringly that her only son was trying to speak to her? There could be no mistake; the mother's perceptions and the time of the accident were verified, corrected for longitude.[9]

Captain Whitfield met another hoodoo in 1889 when he joined the *Dilbhur* at Middlesbrough. She was already 'unlucky' for six weeks earlier she had capsized and drowned three men working in the hold. Then on 1 March as she was towing down the Tees, Whitfield, on watch, saw rapidly approaching lights and a steamer sliced through *Dilbhur* to the waterline. She was leaking like a basket but her crew managed to get her back to port. 'Unfortunate Barque Meets with Second Disaster,' cried the newsvendors' placards. Lugubrious stevedores constantly whispered warnings to the apprentices: 'She's doomed, lads, go home to your Dads. There isn't a rat in the ship. D'you know what that means?' So much for superstition – the ship never suffered another accident of any kind.

To some extent jinxing can be ameliorated. W. R. S. Harris, who sailed in 1906 as a midshipman in the full-rigged wool-clipper *Illawarra*, told of her narrow escape from collision between London and Gravesend. After such a reprieve, in a remnant of magical disguises, it was customary to change the colour scheme of a ship's hull and thus bamboozle the hostile spirits who had marked her for attention. Black topsides with rows of painted ports distinguished Devitt & Moore's vessels: the modified colour scheme called for black above the ports, with a narrow black band below, and grey paint down to the boot-topping.[10]

Scottish fishermen, although of their race and economically-minded, always considered it feckless to use a boat which had capsized with loss of life. Such a vessel was never used again by her home village, although she might be sold to neighbours with perfect safety. To some, only disposal by fire, dramatic and expensive, effectively terminated a sinister boat. After the Broughton Ferry disaster, on 20 March 1960, the ferry-boat, instantly labelled 'jinx', was burned on the foreshore by night and her ashes allowed to wash out to sea on the tide. The custom is not uncommon. At the Belsize boatyard, Southampton, the smashed remains of the third *Morning Cloud* were stripped, cut up and burned. The intention, now merely a nautical tradition, was once purificatory; 'It gets the death out of a boat.'

In lighter mood perhaps, two British yachtsmen at the 1976

Montreal Olympics burned their boat *Gift Horse*, when she failed to achieve a medal. To return the boat to Britain was expensive; local sale, impossible; so skipper Alan Warren and David Hunt set fire to *Gift Horse* with a safety flare. Time polished their tale. Hunt said, 'I stepped out for a smoke, the skipper said "Careful, careful!" and the bloody thing went up . . . call it a crime of passion.' Behind the jokes there seems little doubt that the burning was really the ancient purge of ill-luck. Had *Gift Horse* won a gold medal would she have ended thus?

Sterling ships conveyed comfortable emanations of security and luck. They lost neither spars nor seamen; owners never lacked freights and handsome profits; crews left them with regret; nostalgia accompanied their dissolution. Such was the *John o' Gaunt*, launched in 1835 and skippered by the celebrated Captain John Robertson, whose credentials were such that Canton tea merchants liked to label their teachests 'Per *John o' Gaunt*' for luck, even when consigning them to other bottoms. It was almost an insurance.[11]

Lucky captains made lucky ships. In forty-five years of command Captain William Stuart of the *Loch Etive* (who once sailed from Glasgow to Australia in seventy-two days) lost neither mast nor man overboard. Happy too was the *Alert* to which, in San Diego, Richard Henry Dana transferred from the sinister *Pilgrim*. His impression of the ship was immediately encouraging:

> The men told great stories of her sailing, and had entire confidence in her as a 'lucky ship'. She was seven years old, and had always been in the Canton trade, had never met with an accident of any consequence, nor made a passage that was not shorter than the average. The third mate . . . 'believed in the ship'; and the chief mate thought as much of her as he would of a wife and family.

Luck of this delicately-poised kind was also enjoyed by the *Hippogriffe* of Cape Cod, which, although only of 678 tons, made sturdy voyages round the Horn to San Francisco and Calcutta. Once, in the China Sea, she struck an uncharted rock but worked herself free and made Hong Kong safely. In dry-dock a stone was found to be securely rammed within the hole, sealing it tight against the sea. Had the rock come free the ship would certainly have foundered. *Hippogriffe*'s crew happily endorsed her fortunate name.[12]

'The Manners . . . of a Great Lady'

Empathy between captain and ship is proverbial and old sea-captains are allowed to prefer ships to wives ('A sailor's wife? A widow from her wedding-day!'). Expressing such feelings formally, a Greek skipper 'espouses' his new boat and hangs up a laurel crown, the sign of a shoreside marriage. From first to last the relationship is enduring. The captain remains on board an abandoned ship until all passengers and crew have been taken off. If she sinks before rescue is complete the captain is traditionally expected to go down with his command.

Skippers describe sea-kindly confidantes: 'You have only to *will* her to do something and she responds!' said Captain Parker admiringly of the *Olympic*; Captain Arthur Rostron complimented the *Mauretania*, 'She had the manners and deportment of a great lady and behaved herself as such!' In a letter to Basil Lubbock, Captain John Keay, master of the clipper *Ariel*, the nonpareil, acclaimed the most beautiful ship ever seen, declared, 'It was a pleasure to coach her . . . I could trust her like a thing alive in all evolutions . . . she could do anything short of speaking.' On the naval side, Captain Adkins, RN, was heard to say loyally that during the Napoleonic Wars his patriotic ship – encouraged to even greater efforts by her master's promises of a fresh coat of paint – sailed faster after a ship flying French colours than after any other.

Of the return home of 'dear old *Spray*', affectionate companion on his voyage round the world in 1895-8, Captain Joshua Slocum wrote:

The *Spray* was not quite satisfied till I sailed her around to her birthplace, Fairhaven, Massachusetts, farther along, so on July 3, with a fair wind, she waltzed beautifully round the coast and up the Acushnet River to Fairhaven, where I secured her to the cedar spile driven in the bank to hold her when she was launched. I could bring her no further home.

Every vessel had her little ways. Speaking as one, her crew endowed the famous *Passat* with a soul. She disliked enclosure between cliffs (indeed in narrow waters, she had to be coaxed to obey at all); she also despised tugs. When the Bristol tug came out to meet her a westerly wind blew up, *Passat* suddenly forged ahead and the tug, unable to cast off, struck her side and nearly capsized. The broken tow-wire wound itself round the tug's propeller and, unheeding, the stately *Passat* swept on. History was merely repeating itself, said the crew: off Kotka the tug *had* capsized and eight men were drowned.[13]

The master of the *Herzogin Cecilie* allowed for regular delays in the South Atlantic where, in exactly the same place, the Duchess 'always stopped for a rest', an occurrence confirmed by the log on voyage after voyage. Precisely the same thing had occurred under the German flag. Yet she always relished the *North* Atlantic; a mere twenty-two days once saw her from the Line to the Channel.

Ships transcended mere creatures of wood and iron. The woolclippers, said sailors, knew the road to the Antipodes better than their skippers. There were strange stories of ships making lonely ways home. When *Blue Jacket* was lost by fire near the Falklands in 1869 and her figurehead, miraculously unharmed, was washed up on the coast of Western Australia two years later, old salts declared that the ship 'wanted to complete her passage'. A year after the Battle of the Falkland Islands in

1914, fishermen of the Schleswig coast of Germany sighted a dinghy, empty and waterworn, yet pursuing a perfect course for the German naval base at Cuxhaven. She bore the name *Nürnberg*, one of the German light cruisers sunk during the battle.[14]

Sir Alan Herbert gives the name *Singing Swan* to the Thames sailing-barge which in real life returned alone from the beaches of Dunkirk in June 1940 after her crew, away in their dinghy collecting survivors, had been killed by a bomb. The *Swan*, deserted, unmolested, her topsail set, remained at anchor until at the top of the tide, by singular mix of moon and water, she worked herself free. With anchor dragging she sailed across the Channel through a confusion of mines, wrecks and sandbanks to the Kentish coast, where, undamaged yet quite empty, she anchored herself on Sandwich Flats. And in July 1970 after a towing epic to Bristol (for permanent display in the very berth where she had been built) Richard Goold-Adams, chairman of the project, said of the 3,270-ton *Great Britain*, derelict in the Falklands for a century: 'The *Great Britain* triumphed over all her difficulties – almost as if the old ship *wanted* to come home.'

'Luff, Luff, Hail of Distress . . .'

Remarkable too in its manifestation is the legendary 'captain's sixth sense', described by Commodore Bissett as 'the mental equipment of command', born of enhanced alertness and, it would seem, some more elusive quality.

A famous story tells of the 542-ton barque *Countess of Dufferin*, Captain Doble, master, which left Saint John, New Brunswick, on the final voyage of her twenty-year career on 15 December 1891. Just after Christmas Day a hurricane struck and it soon became clear that, under the crew's feet, the ship was starting to break up. The provision store was swept away; the sea entered the drinking water; the crew, soaked and starving, clung together in the forecastle as the ship settled, her decks awash. Full of wood, she could

The *Great Eastern* in a storm. During building two riveters were said to have been immured in the double hull and the ship's later ill-luck was freely attributed to this

sink no further. With the distressed ensign above them, and more dead than alive, for three days the crew hung on.

Meanwhile the barque *Arlington*, 849 tons, was homeward bound in ballast from Cardiff to New York. On the night of 28 December, Captain Samuel Bancroft Davis, a 'lucky' captain and a thruster, had a compelling dream that he had heard a hail from a ship in distress. So vivid was the picture that he rushed on deck shouting 'Luff, luff, hail of distress!'; the mate and helmsman, hearing nothing, regarded him strangely. He retired below, but again was disturbed, this time by the words 'latitude 52 degrees North, longitude 21 degrees West' ringing in his ears. This was found to be at least a day's sailing north but Captain Davis felt oddly obliged to obey instructions. Course was changed. The mate was told that the captain's dream had shown him the *Arlington*'s boat rescuing a square-rigger's crew and '*You* were in the boat'. The mate was disbelieving: the boat was the second mate's job (he had heard tales of captains going mad). Everyone watched Davis closely. Then, at 3 am on 29 December, wakeful and on deck, Captain Davis heard the to him entirely-expected hail, faint yet unmistakable: '*Countess of Dufferin* – sinking – standby.' At dawn three seamen and Second Mate Andrewson launched the boat but a sudden roll injured Andrewson, and the mate James Hemeon stepped into his place. The captain came off as the sun rose and in the pale light the *Arlington* took her position. Captain Doble was able to report his ship as 'lost at sea, latitude 52° 30′ N, longitude 21° 20′ W'. Davis would make no comment except that 'the Almighty had used him to carry out His wishes'.[15]

With similar prescience Captain Hayward, master of the *Coorong*, in 1891 rescued the crew of the wrecked *Holt Hill* from the uninhabited island of St Paul in the Indian Ocean, after their ship had burned. *Coorong* was bound for Adelaide with a fair wind and no wish to loiter. One afternoon Hayward went below for a nap but could not sleep. 'The question as to whether there was anyone on St Paul's would not leave my mind.' Eventually course was changed and sleep followed; then second thoughts intervened and *Coorong* headed for Cape Leeuwin once more. But again Hayward let instinct win and as the island came into view, with the castaways' fire and flag, a great cheer went up. 'Here you are, and I'm very glad to see you,' was Captain Hayward's cheerful greeting to his thirty-seven starving guests, among them young Lightoller, later the senior surviving officer of RMS *Titanic*.[16]

The Dying Ship

Ideally, the obsequies of a thing so lively as a ship should be ceremonious. Scuttling of old friends far out to sea so that they may rest for ever in their element has much appeal. When the end came for the much-loved *Queen Mary* and later the *Queen Elizabeth* many advocated splendid sinkings in mid-Atlantic, scene of their triumphs, rather than the humiliations of the knacker's yard. In the event the death of the *Queen Elizabeth* was not without drama, if not dignity; and admirers of the *Queen Mary*, regretful that scuttling was not chosen, may find a wry satisfaction in reports from Long Beach,

California, where the ship was taken in 1968 to be the centrepiece of an 'entertainment complex'. The venture has been described in the press as a 'multi-million-dollar fiasco . . . almost as if the old girl is getting back at us. She didn't like being dragged halfway round the world to have her insides pulled out and be turned into a floating Disneyland. There's been a jinx on the whole project.' Financial difficulties and poor attendances have been reported: a state of affairs locally called the '*Queen*'s revenge'.[17]

Privileged ships have been buried at sea. In 1949 the *Implacable*, formerly *Duguay-Trouin*, last survivor of the French fleet that fought at Trafalgar, no longer seaworthy, was towed from her Portsmouth anchorage into the deep Channel and reverently sunk, amid respectful *vales* from the navies of France and Britain.

The great racing yachts reached their apogee in the 1930s and passed away with their patron, King George V, who loved his own big gaff cutter *Britannia*. After his death in 1936 the ship, stripped of historic fittings, was scuttled in the western Channel, in the racing waters she knew so well. Her racing rival, *Westward*, property of the legendary T. B. Davis, went to the same Valhalla. By 1907 the life of the *Thermopylae*, of the great sisterhood of tea-clippers, was closing. Mariners with feeling hearts, the Portuguese owners sank her honourably by naval gunfire in the Bay of Cascais. Elaborate too were the honours paid to the *Ile de France* when she was sold to Japanese breakers in 1959. Before the shipping world, navies, the *corps diplomatique*, under the great bas-relief of the Ile de France, final ceremonies took place at Osaka. Before a Shinto altar, laden with offerings, a priest conducted a purification ceremony which 'cleansed her soul' that she might approach the gods. She was then officially dead.

In another emotional departure the *Mauretania* left Southampton flying a Blue Riband pendant with the dates 1907–29, the remarkable twenty-two years when she held the Atlantic speed record. Nostalgic crowds sang 'Auld Lang Syne', the 'Last Post' rang out, and as she was warped into the Scottish yard, pipers played 'The Flowers of the Forest' as her steam whistles sounded for the last time on shipboard.

If a ship sinks at sea she receives a salute from others present: ensigns are dipped thrice and whistles blow. The *Titanic* survivors doffed their hats as their ship slipped away. And when HMS *Kelly* sank off Crete in 1941 after being divebombed, Captain Lord Louis Mountbatten, RN, called to other survivors round him in the water for 'Three cheers for the old ship!'

Some sailors have favoured ceremonies in Viking style. The Norsemen laid a warrior on a bier upon his ship and with the oar lashed and sails set it became his funeral pyre. Arthurian legend has burial ships; the Egyptians also. North American Indians buried their dead in canoes at sea; so did the Pacific Islanders. On the North Sea's rim some chiefs were buried on land but in their boats, bows toward the sea. Sailors have transposed this attractive idea to the disposal of boats themselves. In September 1976, *Sea Breezes* spoke of 'the best news on the barge front', that the veteran *Westmoreland* was to be rebuilt in Kent. There had been talk of a 'Viking funeral' but 'Genuine wooden sailing vessels are now far too rare for this sort of nonsense.'

3 Phantom Ships and Sailors

Ghost ships sail the seven seas, returning to familiar waters, at whose bottoms they lie and on whose wild and barren lee shores they met their ends. Or are all spectres delusions, fostered by moonlight, dark cliffs and scudding clouds? Tired men staring into storms saw what they wished; a cruiser on a wartime northern sweep signalled at dawn: 'Enemy battleship, bearing NNE distance two miles. Preparing to ram.' And a few minutes later: 'Cancel last signal. Battleship turns out to be lighthouse.' The twin-towered Skaggerak lighthouses have misled unwary eyes. Thus are ghosts born.

For all their savagery, wars have bred few ghosts. Usually ship-phantoms rise from storm and wreck and, glowing with light, decks rotted, crews skeletal, helms untended, they approach silently on collison courses from which with diabolical cunning they swing away, leaving shaken crews to marvel that they lived. It was a moment to stay close to the figurehead, the most protective companion when 'trouble' was expected. Or the ghost might be of the sailor himself. Not every seaman's soul passes easily to its appointed place. Comradeship and loyalties may transcend death and restless shades reappear to warn of danger or to greet shipmates, revisit old scenes, or merely to memorialise themselves: 'One of these nocturnal visitants was supposed to visit our ship . . . you might have seen the most athletic, stouthearted sailor on board, when called to take his night-watch aloft, glancing at the yards and tackling of the ship for the phantom.'

Some, backing sound science, suggest that mirages and 'looming' account for phantoms. When the brig *Barracouta* was surveying in South African waters in 1821, the log of HMS *Severn* (Captain Owen, RN) contained this remarkable entry:

> In the evening of April 6th, when off Port Danger, the *Barracouta* was seen about two miles to leeward. Struck with the singularity of her being so soon after us, we at first concluded that it could not be she; but the peculiarity of her rigging and other circumstances convinced us that we were not mistaken. Nay, so distinctly was she seen that many well-known faces could be observed on deck, looking towards our ship . . . we became surprised that she made no effort to join us, but on the contrary stood away . . . During the night we could not perceive any light or indication of her locality. The next morning we anchored in Simon's Bay, where for a whole week we were in anxious expectation of her arrival . . . but at this very period the *Barracouta* must have been above three hundred miles from us.

Not for nothing are Cape waters the preferred cruising ground of Captain Vanderdecken, the 'Flying Dutchman', where 'spectres' were reported so often that the Admiralty scarcely heeded the *Severn*'s experience. Captain A. T. Mahan, USN, wrote of such mirages on African coasts as 'Cape Flyaways', 'Dutchman's Land' or 'Butterland'.

Some phantoms were undoubtedly wooden derelicts, captives of winds and currents, which hung about the sea-lanes for years. Not until the 1930s when the last were destroyed did 'ghost ships' fall sharply in number. The US Coast Guard knows of one, the *Bayshimo*, which sailed bleak Arctic seas, revealing and concealing herself at the fog's drifting whim. She had gone aground about 1931 near Point Barrow and, abandoned, was carried about by the pack ice. The Eskimos were never distressed by the 'ghost' – when she hove into view they put out at once to snatch what stores they could from her hold.

These are the rational explanations for sea-phantoms. What of the rest? Many laugh, yet old sailors describe sea-events beyond normal experience, and the supernatural can never quite be ruled out. The sea, teasing and treacherous, retains her mystery. Without further comment a selection of sea-ghost stories follows.

Ships of Fire

Legend (contradictory as in most oft-told tales) holds that about 1738 the *Palatine*, in a distressful passage, storm-assaulted and short of food and water, crossed the Atlantic with refugees from Germany. Despairingly her skipper steered for Rhode Island and help. None came. Rather, on 27 December in bitter weather, enticed by wreckers' lanterns, the ship struck Block Island. The passengers struggled ashore and the vessel drifted away to the island's ironbound west coast where the wreckers lifted their final loot before burning the ship, leaving to die in the flames a mad woman who would not leave. Victim of this wretched end, the *Palatine* has returned again and again. Thus wrote Whittier in his poetic reconstruction of the event:

> Down swooped the wreckers, like birds of prey,
> Tearing the heart of the ship away,
> And the dead had never a word to say.
>
> And then, with ghastly shimmer and shine
> Over the rocks and the seething brine,
> They burned the wreck of the 'Palatine' . . . .

> But the year went round, and when once more
> Along their foam-white curves of shore
> They heard the line-storm rave and roar,
>
> Behold! again, with shimmer and shine
> Over the rocks and the seething brine
> The flaming wreck of the 'Palatine'.

Wrecking was a coastal occupation until the nineteenth century – at its mildest, beachcombing; at its nadir, dependent on such monstrous tricks as 'jibber the kibber' or 'Judas lights' – lanterns carried by grazing beasts to entice ships ashore. 'Sea-offerings' were every shore-dweller's birthright. But longshoremen knew that if they burned wood from such wrecks or used it in their homes, they would be tormented by screams and knockings on stormy nights.

On her anniversary the *Palatine*, now a weather-warning, rises and burns, with a light that is 'greenish . . . darting like flames . . . luminous . . . now small . . . now extended like a ship' and,

> Wise sound-skippers, though skies be fine,
> Reef their sails, when they see the sign,
> Of the blazing wreck of the 'Palatine'.

The unimaginative offer reflections of oily menhaden shoals on waterlaid fog as an explanation of the light. Nevertheless the level-headed keepers of the Block Island Light have long told of a burning ship far offshore and of having heard, between blasts of their fog-horn, the lunatic screams of the *Palatine*'s last passenger.

The *Isadore* was lost in 1842, with Captain Leander Foss, all her passengers and crew of fifteen. One Thomas King signed articles, then dreamed thrice of the ship's striking a lee shore and of seven black coffins laid on Kennebunkport quay – and hid in the woods until she sailed. He gained virtue thereby: had he not heeded the Lord's voice? At midnight shore-dwellers heard despairing cries and by morning bodies were washed ashore. Only that of one passenger, Captain G—, could be identified. That morning he had accidentally pulled on his red flannel drawers wrong side out but, saying that this was lucky, refused to change. Only one of his legs was found, still encased in flannel. Now, on the last night of November, the *Isadore* drives again on to leaping breakers, amid drowning cries.

Stories of the *Young Teazer*, a ship which blazes, explodes and vanishes, have enlivened Nova Scotian coastal life for 165 years. The first *Teazer*, a privateer under letters of marque in the war of 1812, was captured and burned by the British navy. Her seamen were imprisoned and her officers, including the first lieutenant, Frederick Johnson, paroled, awaiting exchange under the conventions of war. But unconstrained by honour, Samuel Adams of New York applied on 3 May 1813 for letters of marque for a 124-ton privateer *Young Teazer*, her figurehead a grinning alligator, and to her the ship's company, Johnson commanding, repaired. Her predatory career was brief. She sailed, captured a vessel or two, entered Halifax Harbour, escaped under false colours, and was chased by the *Sir John Sherbrooke*, the *Castor* and the *Manly* before, on 26 June, *La Hogue* trapped her in Mahone Bay as the wind died. Boarding parties prepared but on *Young Teazer* Lieutenant Johnson was seen to enter the cabin with a redhot coal in his hand and, under the watchers' horrified gaze, the ship flew apart in a sheet of flame. Johnson, rightly surmising that he would swing, had fired the magazine. *La Hogue* found few survivors.

Lunenburg fishermen have often seen the '*Teazer*-light', a 'ball of fire' burning for minutes, in gloom or fog, at sunset or moonset, a darkling forerunner of storms. *Young Teazer* approaches ships at sea before veering away in flames. Giving the lie to those who say that her viewers die before the year is out is one man who has seen the light 'as often as I have fingers and toes'. When *Teazer* burns the superstitious stay on shore.

The Flying Dutchman

The crowded fleet of ghosts fades beside the *Flying Dutchman*, most enduring of all ships of legend, condemned to rove the oceans imperilling all whose eyes fall upon her:

> But Heaven help the ship near which the demon sailor steers!
> The doom of those is sealed, to whom the Phantom Ship appears,
> They'll never reach their destin'd port, they'll see their homes no more.
> They who see the *Flying Dutchman*, never, never, reach the shore.

sang Boyles O'Reilly in *Songs of Southern Seas*.

Northern European folk-myth supplies the *Dutchman*'s origins (the name is applied to both captain and ship); the Jew wandering in retribution for slighting Christ; murderous Count von Falkenburg, sailing ever northward, dicing with Satan for his soul; Odin's Wild Hunt of the sky. Bowing to fact, some believe the *Dutchman* to be the real-life mariner Bernard Fokke, whose iron-encased masts ensured that no crew's importunacy compelled him to reduce sail and who bargained with the Devil to reach the East Indies in ninety days. For such temerity he was condemned to sail eternally the waters of the Southern Capes in *Libera Nos* – black flag silver-spangled with death's-heads and flames whipping at the masthead, and on deck Fokke, counting off weary centuries on an hourglass. Or the *Dutchman* is Vanderdecken, Tromp's contemporary, who 'snapped his fingers at God and the Devil', blasphemy punished by eternal sailing, usually, but not inevitably, round Capes Stiff and Storm.

Proclaiming tempest, death or madness, this restless ship is visible in the glooming before storms of which she is the premonitor. Luminous, black-hulled, without food, water or hope, the *Dutchman* races past in the yeasty smother of high green seas, 'unblest of God and man'. Her *mise en scène* is among treacherous waters, frosted by moonlight, befogged in bright airs, masts fiery at night; her crew, rejected plague-bearers in every port.

The prudent do not hail her nor answer her hails, or indeed those of any ghost ship. To do so led to false courses, embayment, lee shores. Vanderdecken shrieks of letters – woe to those who listen! Such correspondence becomes dust and bestows nothing but misfortune. The vision of the Unspeakable Wanderer sours wine and turns food to beans – the old sailor's bugbear. No coast was exempt from her presence. In Galveston Bay, Texas, in 1892 she was seen twice. 'Nearly run down by her,' reported one shaken master; while the Norwegian *Fair Hilda*'s master viewed a luminescent vessel casting no shadow as she stormed past. His crew saw nothing.

At Cape Town in March 1857 were landed survivors from the *Joseph Somers* which had on 29 February, off Tristan da Cunha, suffered a disastrous encounter with the Scourge of Southern Seas. Ready with chilling depositions was a still-agitated party. As the *Flying Dutchman* sailed right under the *Somers*' bow, they descried on the poop Vanderdecken himself, dirty white curls streaming, moon-face a mask of malevolence, eyes like hot coals, yellow teeth a-snarl, debating whether to board the *Joseph Somers* – or to blast her to perdition! With a final sneer of loathing, Vanderdecken swung his ship aside, and through a clammy blue fog passengers heard ghastly laughter which filled all with dread. The encounter lasted minutes; hours later the passengers still shuddered at the recollection.

Soon the first smoke wreathed its way across the deck. The fast-moving fire's cause was mysterious: a falling lamp? or Vanderdecken's work? The demoralised passengers, consumed by fatalism, fought the flames half-heartedly and were soon driven to the last unsinged corner of the deck. Only *Nimrod*'s providential appearance saved them from roasting alive.[18]

The Royal Navy met the *Dutchman* more than once. The log of the *Bacchante*, cruising in the Pacific, contained the story:

July 11, 1881. During the middle watch the *Flying Dutchman* crossed our bows. She first appeared as a strange, red light, as of a ship all aglow, in the midst of which light the masts, spars and sails, seemingly those of a normal brig, some two hundred yards distant from us, stood out in strong relief as she came up. The look-out man on the forecastle reported her as close on the port bow, where also the officer of the watch from the bridge clearly saw her, as did also the quarter-deck midshipman, who was sent forward at once to the forecastle to report back. But on arriving there, no vestige nor any sign . . . of any material ship was to be seen . . . The early morning, as the night had been, was clear, the sea strangely calm.

During the forenoon the *Dutchman*'s customary spite began to make itself felt. From the foretopmast the seaman who had reported the phantom fell to his death: '. . . A smart royalyard seaman, one of the most promising hands in the ship, and every man on board feels sad and despondent at his loss.' Then, as the squadron entered port, the commander, apparently in perfect health, was taken acutely ill and died almost at once.[19]

Vice-Admiral Gordon Campbell, VC, famous for his service in World War I 'mystery ships' (heavily-armed and disguised decoy merchantmen) also had a story to unfold. He had just taken command of the *Dunraven*, appearing as a 'Blue Funnel' steamer, and was on passage from Plymouth to Gibraltar. The men were yarning in the galley. 'I've heard of the Phantom Ship in the Bay of Biscay before,' said one, 'but I never believed it till I and several others saw her this afternoon. There she was on our starboard beam, when suddenly she vanished. Bad sign – something happens to the ship that sights her, so I'm told.' 'Coming events cast their shadow . . .' said his friend sagely. A wireless operator near the door joined in: 'It's funny you should be talking like this. I've had a feeling all day that I'm going to be wounded, and I've gone out of my way to have a good bath, so as to be nice and clean if anything happens.' The other operator said he had done the same. 'Whether by coincidence or not,' wrote Admiral Campbell, 'the man who had spoken of coming events was mortally wounded in action the very next day and both wireless operators were seriously wounded.'[20]

The *Dutchman* even frightened U-boat crews of World War II. Admiral Karl Dönitz, Commander-in-Chief of the German Navy, wrote that certain of his submarine crews had seen the *Dutchman* 'or some other so-called ghost ship on duty east of Suez. The men said they preferred the strength of the Allied Fleet in the North Atlantic to the terror of a second meeting with the phantom'. The story wears so well that even today's worldly mariners are jokingly half-prepared for a sighting. A few years ago, Ernest Gann, on passage from Madeira to Barbados and lying becalmed without oil for the auxiliary motor of the *Albatros* sent a hurried radio call to a vessel on the horizon, asking if an eastbound tanker with a becalmed sailing ship in view, would acknowledge. From the radio boomed the cheerful reply, 'Tanker Arndale! Good morning! We thought we were looking at a *Flying Dutchman*!'[21]

The Ship Swallower

The supernatural marks caused by the tempest which battered England's coasts on 19 November 1703 still overlie each other in sad confusion. On this despairing night the Royal Navy alone lost thirteen ships, driven to their deaths on the Goodwin Sands, off the Kentish coast, declared by Shakespeare to be 'A very dangerous flat, and fatal, where the carcasses of many a tall ship lie buried.' Projecting masts are poignant reminders of past accidents. Legend makes these swirling quicksands – ten miles long, submerged at high and partly exposed at low tide, defiant of hydrographers – the once fruitful 'Isle of Lomea', changed by eleventh-century storms. The unthinking dismiss night cries round this prime sea-hazard as 'gulls'; the perceptive recognise the voices of many victims.

During the increasing fury of the Great Storm, British

The 'Great Storm' in the Downs, 1703, when the Royal Navy alone was said to have lost thirteen ships on the Goodwin Sands. Several maritime ghost stories date from this storm

warships making for the Medway sought the traditional safety of the Downs anchorage between Deal and the Sands; but, in the wind's mounting fury, they dragged their anchors and struck the Goodwins. Among those lost were the *Northumberland* and the *Mary*. Survivors were few but one achieved a strange vision on that wild night: 'A great warship of Drake's day, her sails tattered, on fire from fore to aft, her guns firing, served by half-demented sailors, bore down upon us, sailed right through our ship, finally vanished before our eyes into the depths of the Sands.' Was the half-drowned witness battered into delirium or did the intense emotions in his battle for life evoke a response from others who had suffered in the same waters long before? Was the ghost an Armada fugitive from the Battle of Gravelines? Or the Spanish galleon hard-driven in the same fight which Richard Hakluyt described? A junior officer of this ship, aghast at imminent surrender, felled his captain and was himself instantly hanged. Fighting broke out and in moments of professional negligence the blazing ship struck the Sands. Her crew fired their guns in distress as she broke up.

Near the memorial date, fifty years later, on 28 November 1753, an East Indiaman's captain logged another wraith. He was riding out bad weather off the Sands when driving down on him he saw an armed frigate. A collision seemed inevitable and the first officer was about to slip the anchor when the stranger's name became clear – *Northumberland*! She appeared to be unmanageable, her masts gone, hull damaged, as she cleared the East Indiaman by two ships' lengths and, firing her guns, disappeared into a black haze. As she passed, the horrified watchers saw men leaping into the sea, but they made no sound as they hit the water: 'My men, as I, were nigh dead with horror of it all.'

In fair winds, on 13 February 1748 (some say in 1724), the *Lady Luvibund* shaped a promising course down Channel for Oporto with her cargo and, more importantly, Captain Simon Reed's new bride, Annetta, her mother and their wedding guests. But vengeful for the loss of his intended, Mate John Rivers brained the helmsman and ran the sailing-ship on to the Sands. The merry party in the cabin, deaf to imminent destruction, was finally roused by sounds of pounding seas, snapping timbers and Reed's idiot laughter as the *Luvibund* was drawn down. Rivers' mother later remembered her son's long-pondered vengeance 'even though it cost him his life'.

The *Lady Luvibund* did not rest. Fifty years later, on 13 February 1798, Captain James Westlake of the *Edenbridge*, warily passing the Sands, was nearly run down by an unidentified sailing-ship which in proper spectral manner sheered nimbly past, to shouts of drunken laughter from below. Westlake found that local fishermen, sufficiently persuaded of her substance to search for survivors, had found nothing. In 1848 the 'hovellers' of Deal (*inter alia* fishermen, smugglers and salvagers) again remarked the stranger and put out to her aid. No trace was found. Again without physical clue she was seen on 13 February 1898. The superstitious waited for 1948. But, disappointingly, in that memorial year the *Lady Luvibund* remained invisible, although in a far-fetched attempt to match her with the supernatural at all costs, some discovered her hand in the wreck of the *Silvia Onorato* on the Goodwins, saying that instead of making a personal appearance she had claimed a sacrifice.

A modern mystery and ghost arose from the loss in January 1857 of the mail steamer *Violet*, bound from Ostend to Dover on a fearsome night of wind and driven snow. The North Goodwins light-vessel saw the little ship strike the Sands in a towering arc of spray, and at once fired rockets and cannon. When the tug *Aid* arrived from Ramsgate a dawn search revealed nothing more than the mailbags in the sea, three corpses lashed to a lifebuoy and the *Violet*'s mast sticking up from the wet sand. Of her crew of eighteen and her single passenger no further signs were found. The wreck made sixteen wives widows and left forty-three children fatherless.

The tale was taken up ninety years later when, on 1 January 1947, George Carter, looking across stormy waters from his light-vessel, saw a steamer plunging straight for the Sands in the yellow gleam of rockets. The lifeboat was called out but after hours of searching the grim report was of no trace of vessel or crew; the men finally concluded that they had witnessed a memorial re-enactment of the *Violet*'s wreck. Such mysteries continue: on 24 October 1939, the German submarine *U-16* was discovered stranded on the Goodwins with, says one local legend, every man of her crew inexplicably dead at his post.

Every coast has its ghosts. In misty weather the Gold Rush clipper *Tennessee* again rides quietly near San Francisco's Golden Gate Bridge; the Belgian steamer *Concordia* sails the North Sea; Captain Kidd's *Quedah Merchant* appears in ghostly combat in Long Island Sound. Some believe that Kidd still patrols America's east coast in moonlight, landing to inspect his many treasure caches, guarded by the ghosts of defunct pirates. The selection of the 'watcher' was macabre. As the chests were buried the captain asked 'Who will guard these?' and a man anxious for personal gain proposed himself.

Later that night when he was hopelessly drunk he was buried alive with the treasure. Pirates swore by such guardians.

A long-forgotten Channel sea-fight is commemorated in autumn fog by crashes of gunfire and falling masts. And at Cap d'Espoir, Gulf of St Lawrence, redcoats crowd the decks, drums beat to quarters and an officer and his lady stand pointing on the quarterdeck, as a brilliantly lighted British man-of-war, said to be the flagship of those sent by Queen Anne to attack the French forts, strikes the cliffs before sinking into transparent waters.

In sharp contrast to these ghosts of history is another, in its way more moving – an oil slick, an iridescent rug among the dolphins and amberjacks, riding the Gulf Stream off Cape Hatteras. Captain Ernal Foster, a local skipper, remembers that it first appeared in 1942 when Allied losses of tankers and freighters off this coast were grievously heavy. On every day of every year since, the slick has been seen and smelt in and about the Cape currents and local sailors say that it will endure for ever, a perpetual war memorial.[22]

Quiet Hauntings

Drama is often the sea-phantom's prerogative but some ghosts are the more memorable for their quietness. Rowing home one evening from Steel's Cove to Bear Cove, Nova Scotia, a pilot found himself quietly pacing, for nearly three hours, a four-oared gig manned by silent ghosts, whose oars almost touched his as ghosts and living rowed stroke for stroke.

The *Royal George*, the *Mary Rose* and the *Eurydice* are among the many vessels which have foundered in or near Spithead, the sea's arm between Portsmouth and the Isle of Wight. Yet there seem few ghosts. Robert Sutherland Horne, an authority on Portsmouth, knows of only one (if indeed it is a ghost at all). He and two friends were sailing back from Seaview one October evening with a good breeze on the quarter, and were in the triangle formed by Fort Gilkicker, Southsea Castle and Portsmouth Harbour mouth; the holiday season was over; the festoons of summer lights on Southsea front were darkened. A sail crossed their bow, making for the harbour, and they found themselves overtaking, yards apart, what looked like a Viking boat with only one man visible, crouched up aft steering. Her dark squaresail was aglow as though lighted from below by a lantern. The party called a friendly 'Good night!' but the stranger, so near and contrary to custom, did not reply and was lightly dismissed as an 'unsociable blighter!'. They sailed on, concentrating on getting their boat in and up the slipway which took a good hour. Watch was kept for the stranger, for, with the prevailing wind and tide, she had no choice but to follow them. But she never came in; and none knew of any boat of her description.[23]

In August 1910, Rowley W. Murphy, the marine artist and Great Lakes historian, with his father and cousin, was cruising on Lake Ontario. They anchored their yawl for the night in a moon-dappled creek at Etobicoke, near a group of other yachts, and all turned in early. At half past one Murphy was awakened by four blasts of a ship's whistle and putting his head out saw a steamer, flooded with moonlight, about half a mile off shore and heading WSW at about half speed. She had little steam although her chime whistle was loud; her deck and cabin lights had the gentle luminescence of oil lamps; her tall masts carried gaff and brailed up mainsail. For some ten minutes the melodious whistle was heard; by now everyone was awake and watching, and a crew of four set out in a dinghy to give what help they could.

But when they reached the spot where the steamer had sailed there was nothing to see but brilliant moonlight, and a few sleepy gulls. And something that could not be ignored. The water was scored by long gleaming ripples curving away in a moon-touched circle; perhaps the last manifestation of a lake steamer which had foundered a century before on a night of similar beauty.[24]

A happily commemorative ghost of the Pacific arose from the poignant last cruise in 1920 of the old windjammer *Annie E.* of Honolulu. She was so old and worn that only her timber cargo kept her afloat; finally she leaked so alarmingly that her crew abandoned her, leaving only the captain and two seamen on board. She was searched for and almost given up for lost when a steamer saw her fleetingly and then, using intimate knowledge of winds and tides, Captain Erickson of the US Lighthouse Service's *Kukui* caught up with her eight days later. Telling a sea-tale of flashing storms and starvation, hopes fulfilled and frustrated, her captain pleaded for a tow; to him *Annie E.* was both life and fortune. Great efforts were made and *Annie E.* was soon making two knots. But at midnight the old ship broached to and remained thus, despite every endeavour to bring her head up. First Officer Jensen went across and came off with a woeful story; her hawsepipe and side had pulled away; she could go no further and she could not sink. At about noon on 18 August they set fire to her.

But, as befitted a ship of such personality and courage, *Annie E.* did not depart readily for the 'port of lost ships'. Despite events suggesting precisely the contrary, her history is not yet over. At least three ships in Hawaiian waters in recent years have reported encounters in August dawns with a new and youthful white-winged windjammer, in a cloud of canvas, leaning away before a fine breeze, with across her stern, in gleaming gold, the legend '*Annie E.* of Honolulu'.

Forerunners

A sailor is ever in communion with his home; to him, letters, keepsakes and the words 'homeward bound' have special meaning. It is not surprising that a drowned sailor's new-made ghost comes as a 'forerunner' to warn his family of his end. In North Germany such visitants or 'gongers' appear at twilight in the clothes they were wearing when they died, leaving a sad trail of water and seaweed as they step through the bereaved house.

The *locus classicus* of nautical forerunners concerns a Royal Navy officer and a tragedy of all time – the collision off Beirut on 22 June 1893 between the *Victoria*, flagship of the

Mediterranean fleet, and the *Camperdown*. In a sea smooth as glass the British fleet, in two columns of line ahead, received orders from Vice-Admiral Sir George Tryon to invert the line, the leading ships turning towards each other. But although the turning circle of the *Victoria* was some 600 yards, that of the *Camperdown* was distinctly greater; the evolution was dangerous, if not impossible. Vice-Admiral Tryon, a highly-experienced officer, was feared by juniors for his swift tongue and while the order was diffidently questioned amendment came too late. At speed, the *Camperdown*'s ram crashed into the *Victoria* which sank almost immediately with grave loss of life, including that of Tryon himself. He refused a lifebelt, made no attempt to save himself and at the last was heard to murmur, 'It was all my fault'. At the court martial Tryon was held culpable but so strange and disastrous a lapse of judgement was never explained.

Thus arose the best known of all naval ghost stories, once the sensation of the Fleet: also on 22 June, Lady Tryon held a summer 'at home' at her London home in Eaton Square. Most knew that the admiral was at sea and it was therefore with pleasurable surprise that several guests saw what they took to be his figure descend the stairs as though in welcome – some indeed insisted that he paused to speak to them. When questioned, Lady Tryon replied a little shortly that her husband was not expected back; she did not appear to see his apparition herself. At the moment of his London appearance, Admiral Tryon was already at the bottom of the Mediterranean.

Folklore accretions soon formed round the story. *Victoria*'s recommissioning on Good Friday the thirteenth, was remembered; thousands of Syrians from the Bay of Tripoli were said to have witnessed the accident, attracted by a local fakir's exciting pronouncement that 'Allah will visit the ships of the infidels'. And within two hours of the sinking, huge crowds gathered about the dockyard gates in Malta, warned of disaster by some obscure tribal intuition.

In England on 22 June, Lieutenant Reginald H. Bacon, RN, continued technical discussions with fellow officers over lunch after a morning observing torpedo trials at the Whitehead Torpedo Works, Weymouth. Suddenly, with a loud crack, the stem of a wineglass snapped. Someone remarked lightly, 'That should mean a big naval disaster,' recollecting the belief that even to permit a glass to ring sounds some sailor's death knell. Later it was realised that the *Victoria* had sunk at this very moment.

Humbler families too have received warnings. A pillow lovingly sewn by his wife was carried to sea by a sailor from Victoria Beach, Nova Scotia, and when the ship foundered all were lost, but the pillow, remaining obstinately afloat, travelled twenty miles *against* the tide and was washed up near the man's home. It was found by his wife, who felt an inexplicable compulsion to visit the beach. In Cornwall, rocking dairy pans of milk, agitated as the waves of the sea, warned a farmer's wife of the loss of her sailor son. A drowned sailor (now a gull) fluttered against the window of his Breton cottage with the dread message, and a Nova Scotia woman who heard an 'awful squash' across her window knew of her husband's end. Had not 'the waves come to tell her'?

Maine folk tell another perplexing tale. In January 1877 the *N. T. Hill* left Rangoon for Bucksport, Maine, with a cargo of rice. One night at Brewer, about twenty miles from Bucksport, one Zenas Lawry was awakened by a shout of 'Help!' ringing in his ears and saw the deathly pale and soaking wet figure of his neighbour Ephraim Thurston, a blanket about his shoulders, one hand, blue with cold, resting feebly on the bedstead. 'What's the trouble, Ephraim?' gasped Zenas, but without reply the vision faded, leaving only the soughing wind of a stormy dawn. At breakfast his story was laughingly dismissed by his wife as a 'dawn dream'. Everyone assumed that the *N. T. Hill* must have arrived at Bucksport; she had not; nor was she ever seen again. But it was found that a typhoon had swept the Bay of Bengal on the very night of Zenas Lawry's dream.[25]

The Brotherhood of the Sea

Sea-comradeship is sometimes as supportive in death as in life and strange stories tell of the dead bringing help to stricken shipmates. In the cabin of a schooner winter fishing off George's Bank, New England, was discovered a tall, well-built man, who, although a stranger to the crew, was familiarly writing on the slate log at the chart-table. The small vessel had been at sea for weeks: a stowaway was impossible. The skipper, finally induced to enter the cabin, found it empty – but on the *underside* of the slate log were the words: 'Change course to NNE. Steer five hours. Capsized vessel.' Reflecting on the handwriting before him and rejecting any thought of a jest on the part of his largely illiterate crew, the captain obeyed instructions. They took him directly to the capsized vessel, still afloat with sixteen of her crew clinging to her. All were saved. One seaman had been drowned at the moment of capsizing. He was the writer at the cabin table.

Americans spoke of a long-dead captain who returned to supervise changes of course, sitting at ease in his old chair on the poop. In another ship the hand who went aloft to stow the royals always found that 'Old Bill', long deceased, in true shipmately fashion had preceded him. Almost unbearably, American men-of-war's-men of the 1840s felt certain that the voice of a man hanged at the yardarm would be heard that night returning the hail.

In England Sir Francis Drake and his side-drum, said to have beaten his crew to quarters during the Armada fight of 1588 and to have gone round the world with him in 1577–80, enjoy a unique place in folk-legend. It tells that Drake, when dying of yellow fever in 1596 off Porto Bello, instructed that the drum be returned to England, promising that if it were beaten at time of peril he would come again to England's aid. As Sir Henry Newbolt sang in 'Drake's Drum' (1895):

If the Dons sight Devon, I'll quit the port o' Heaven
An' drum them up the Channel as we drummed them long ago.

Many West-countrymen, expressing a natural disbelief that so vigorous a spirit could be finally quenched, are disposed to believe that Drake has already returned, several times, as a man of his time – as Admiral Robert Blake, Lord Nelson, and later as such formidable fighters as Captain F. J. Walker, DSO, RN, who led the Second Escort Group in the Battle of the Atlantic.

Then the story changed. It was said that the drum would beat of its own accord if England's fate hung in the balance. Its beat was heard before Trafalgar, after the declaration of war in 1914, at Jutland, during the Dunkirk evacuation and the Battle of Britain in 1940, and when invasion seemed imminent. In 1918 when the German High Seas Fleet was sailing to surrender, Captain John Luce, OBE, RN, of the escorting *Royal Oak* (with many Devonians in her company) heard a stately drumbeat within his ship. Messengers found no drum and no cause; every man was at action stations; but the sound ceased only when the German ensign was hauled down. As Captain Luce wrote later to Sir Henry Newbolt, 'Was this Drake's Drum?'[26]

A most welcome sailor shade came to the side of Captain Joshua Slocum. He left Boston on 24 April 1895, called at the Azores for bread, butter, vegetables, plums and a white Pico cheese, the gift of the American consul, and then sailed on. But by nightfall he lay helpless and in great pain on the cabin floor. Suddenly, looking up the companionway, he saw at the helm a stranger in foreign rig, a large red cap 'cock-billed' over his ear. 'Señor,' said the stranger, doffing the cap, 'I am one of Columbus's crew. I am the pilot of the *Pinta*, come to aid you. Lie quiet, señor captain, and I will guide your ship tonight.' When Slocum struggled on deck next morning he found the decks 'white as sharks' teeth' from the sweep of the seas; *Spray* was heading as he had left her, having made ninety miles in rough seas through the night, and was still going like a racehorse. Columbus himself could not have held her more closely on course. In his dreams Slocum seemed to see the pilot again – 'I woke with the feeling that I have been in the presence of a friend and seaman of vast experience.' Overboard, as the pilot advised, went the plums – 'You did wrong, captain, to mix cheese with plums . . .' As he approached St Helena on the homeward road, Slocum, again conscious of his companion, 'reached for a bottle of port-wine . . . and took a long pull from it to the health of my invisible helmsman – the pilot of the *Pinta*'.

Memorials

Some manifestations seem to have no purpose other than classic commemoration. On America's east coast the story of the *Charles Haskell* has been told in song and verse for over a century. On her maiden voyage on 6 March 1869, the schooner, skippered by Captain Clifford Curtis of Gloucester, Massachusetts, sailed to fish on George's, but that night the sea got up, anchors dragged and *Haskell* struck another ship which sank like a stone. Of her crew no trace could be found but she was finally identified as the *Andrew Jackson* of Salem, one of nine boats lost on George's that night. To Curtis's pain and anger, several of his crew accused him of having 'blood on his hands' and left his employ.

A week later a Portuguese member of the crew, Manuel Fernández, and Oscar Roihards, on midnight watch, saw a group forrard whom they at first took to be the earlier watch not yet turned in. But Fernández, with the perception of his race, realised that they were not of *Haskell*'s crew. As they watched, a man in dripping oilskins climbed over the rail to join the group, then another, and another; shadowy shapes were joining the ship from every side, and the ghosts, blind to the living, turned to the work of wheel, halyards and nets:

> Right o'er our rail there clambered, as silent one by one
> A dozen dripping sailors, just wait till I am done,
> Their faces pale and sea wet, shone ghostly through the night,
> Each sailor took his station as though he had a right . . .

Twenty-four hours later the ghosts again appeared and remained until the *Charles Haskell*, fishing completed, turned for Gloucester:

They moved about before us till land came into sight,
Or rather I should say, the lighthouse beamed its light,
And then those ghostly sailors moved to the rail again
And vanished in a moment, before the sons of men.

By now none save Manuel Fernández would sail in the accursed vessel. He very sensibly suggested that on the next trip the *Haskell* should be taken into Salem *before* Gloucester 'to take the ghosts home'. But Curtis insensitively disagreed and, unmannable, the *Charles Haskell* lingered for months until her sale to a Nova Scotian who resolved never to take the boat to George's again. As far as is known he never did. The haunting ceased.

Backtracking of a similar kind disposed of a ghost in Captain Joseph Conrad's *Otago*, an iron barque of 345 tons whose previous captain, John Snadden of Wallaroo, had died on board in December 1887, off the Gulf of Siam, and was buried at sea. Conrad took command at Bangkok on 24 January 1888 and cleared for Australia laden with teak. Twenty-one painful days of sailing saw them only 800 miles ahead, at Singapore; all except the cook were ill. Snadden, part-owner of the ship and a Scot, had behaved eccentrically for months, at the end ordering the ship, without cargo, ballast or water to beat up to Hong Kong in fierce monsoons. Before he could be persuaded to turn back, sails were blown away and the crew frightened and exhausted. Soon afterwards he died. Said the chief mate: 'He would have taken the ship down with him if it had been in human power . . . he never meant to see home again . . . he meant to have gone wandering about the world until he lost her with all hands.' Not surprisingly this tormented man left a mark. Difficulties and illness in the ship never ceased. The mate insisted that the ship would be bedevilled until the position where Snadden had been buried was again passed. He was proved to be perfectly correct. The evil influence then vanished.[27]

'Keep Away, Keep Away!'

Assaulted by every gale, guarding dangerous and remote sea-hazards, lighthouses are natural magnets for folklore. Of Minots Ledge Light, on the Cohasset Rocks, Massachusetts, there are many tales. The stability of the lighthouse, built in 1850, soon caused concern; then in April 1851 horrified shore-dwellers heard the fog-bell pounding in distress all night long, until the sounds ceased – the tower and keepers were seen to crash into tumultuous seas. When in 1860 a second lighthouse was built, its keepers quickly noticed that lamp and lens were being carefully polished – although not by them; and later, before gales, the ghost of a lost keeper, Joseph Antoine, was seen grasping the lighthouse ladder as the surf raged past him, calling over and over again 'Keep away, keep away!'

Another long-gone keeper completed ghostly duties at St Simon's Light, Brunswick Harbour, Georgia. In 1907, Keeper George Svendson and his wife – and their dog Jinx – moved in to tend the light. As she heard her husband descending the stairs from the lamp-room every evening, Mrs Svendson set dinner on the table, but one evening when the footsteps reached the ground she realised that Svendson was still aloft. Over the years, both heard the ghostly keeper clattering down the stairs many times and were so unperturbed – even affectionate towards him – that they spent forty years at St Simon's. But the miserable dog always hid whenever the ghost was heard.

Romantic rather than distressing is Savannah's 'Waving Girl'. In 1887 Florence Martus, sister of the keeper of Elba Island Light in the Savannah River, was wooed by a naval lieutenant, who promised to return to marry her. She declared: 'When your ship sails by I'll wave farewell with my apron and when you come back I'll still be waving to you.' Weeks passed, months and years. He never returned. But Miss Martus had begun to wave a greeting to every passing ship; passengers and crews eagerly lined the rails to watch for her, ships whistled in reply to her wave. When George Martus retired in 1931, Florence, a legend in her own lifetime, had been waving to ships for forty-four years. She died long ago and the light is no longer manned, but some Savannah sailors swear that they are still welcomed home by Savannah's 'Waving Girl'.

In 1900 the vengeful spirits of drowned lobstermen were blamed by many for the extraordinary disappearance without trace of three keepers from Eilean More Lighthouse in the Outer Hebrides. And emotions far older than World War I added to the Cornish fear of certain 'beckoning bays' which 'drew' ships to destruction. Like wreckers of old, sailors killed by U-boat attackers were said to have returned in force in 1919 to show false lights in Cornish coves to 'draw' German ships – other flags passed by unseeing – to their doom.

Rudyard Kipling found a similar belief when he visited the British Fleet in 1915. From the skippers of the Trawler and Auxiliary Fleet (many of them Scots) he heard that German submarines, found sunk by means never explained, had been lured to vengeful destruction by the souls of women, such as the 'Ladies of the *Lusitania*', whose deaths they had caused by torpedo attacks on innocent passenger vessels.

4 Talismans and Taboos

'Fore-topman' wrote of service in 'Old Ironsides', 1839–41:

> . . . sailors are generally the most superstitious beings in existence . . . since my sojourn on the boundless ocean, I have never seen an accident occur on shipboard but what someone would step up with prophetic countenance, and engross the attention of every bystander with a relation of some little circumstance that he had taken notice of prior to the occurrence, which he considered as a forewarning . . .

Today superstition may be acknowledged more backhandedly but no less emphatically. The Royal Navy submarine *Osiris* carries the number S13; the boat's tie, with dolphins and thirteen motifs, may be worn only by crew members who dive in *Osiris* at 1300 hours on Friday the thirteenth, the day the submarine completed her successful acceptance trials. 'Anything connected with thirteen turns out right for us,' said Lieutenant Rick Williams, Canadian Forces (Navy), the *Osiris*'s sonar officer.

Distinguished sailors confess to partiality in luck-bringers. Captain Mortimer Hehir, master of the *Queen Elizabeth II*, noticed the local pilot nervously fingering a string of bright green beads as he took the ship through the Bosphorus. 'As we entered the Black Sea the pilot gave a big sigh of relief, handed the beads to me and said, "This is a terribly big ship. I reckon you need these more than me." Now I regard them as a good-luck charm and will always keep them.' Admiral Max Horton, C-in-C Western Approaches in World War II, thought so highly of a ring given to him on the day he joined the Royal Navy's submarine service that he vowed it should never leave his finger. And Winston Churchill sent HMS *Churchill*, named after the first Duke of Marlborough, 'one of his handwritten letters for your Ward Room for luck'. Commodore Irving gave St Christopher all the credit for the *Queen Mary*'s safe docking at New York during a strike in 1938: 'When I realised that I should have to bring her in alone, I took the St Christopher from my pocket and asked the saint, "Can we do it?" He said "Of course!"'

Fate would not be gainsaid. Damage to old friends presaged the worst. The sole decoration in Rear-Admiral Sir Christopher Cradock's cabin in HMS *Good Hope* was a cracked piece of cloisonné which he explained he had carried for luck since early days on the China station. But in 1914 during a hurried change of ship he dropped it. Cradock himself incorrectly interpreted the mishap as meaning that he would *not* come up with the German Fleet – a misfortune to a fighting officer. In fact the accident gave warning of his heroic death at the Battle of Coronel.

Sailors' gold ear-rings, in pierced ears, still bring luck and cure weak eyes and rheumatism. The caul or 'holy hood', a membrane occasionally covering a child's head at birth, has long been cherished by seafarers as an amulet, perhaps because it appears to save the child from 'drowning' in the womb. Even today a caul may change hands for surprising sums. Told that his confidence in his caul was 'a vulgar error', one nineteenth-century veteran who kept it sewn up in his canvas trousers, growled, 'A vulgar error saving from Davy Jones is as good as any other'. No ship carrying a caul could sink. Captain James Bissett, commanding HMS *Roebuck* on Channel patrol in World War I, sent his first lieutenant to investigate a derelict tramp steamer. The officer came off with documents and an envelope boldly labelled 'Our Little Darling's Caul', which mystified everyone until the chief engineer explained. The steamer's crew, who had abandoned ship prematurely, landed safely in Dorset where the master was delighted to regain a valued possession.

Coal from the high tide line as a pocket amulet ensures that the sailor too will be safely washed up on the beach. As on land, horseshoes and hot cross buns were useful. Horseshoes, of sacred iron, made by the smith (always a man of magic), in occult lunar shape, were nailed to masts or under decks. HMS *Victory* is said to have worn one at Trafalgar. Hot cross buns, of holy Good Friday reputation, were long-lasting charms against storm and shipwreck. Also, it was the seaman's fancy to touch his sweetheart's 'bun' or pudenda for luck before sailing.

A right boot fished up is nailed to the mast for luck, but a left boot, vaguely unlucky like all things sinistral, quickly goes back. A shoe thrown after a departing fisherman produces catches; well-wishers remembered that at Whitby, Yorkshire, about 1850, their party gathered at the pier-head to pelt with old boots the boats departing for the annual Greenland fishery. Garlic (strong odours nullify hostile magic) hangs in Turkish fishing-boats against witchcraft, and old nets draped over Chinese junks trap prowling spirits. Until the 1840s naturally-holed 'hagstones', related to *oculi*, hung beneath the gunwales of Dorset fishing-boats; no witch touched a boat thus marked. 'Lucky' fiddle-fish are, if plentiful, nailed copiously over lockers and bunks of North Sea trawlers or towed astern of the vessel.

Such amulets are widely known and used but some crews had equal faith in those particular to their vessel alone. At three of the major actions of World War I HMS *New Zealand* escaped serious damage and all casualties, phenomenal luck attributed by her crew to a Maori *piu-piu* and *tiki* worn in action by her captain.

In 1913 the ship, presented to the British Government by

the people of New Zealand, visited the Dominion, and among many gifts received a greenstone *tiki* or pendant and a *piu-piu* or flax kilt about 18in long with a waistband. These were presented to her commanding officer, Captain Lionel Halsey, RN, by a Maori chief, with the request that he should always wear them in action and the promise that, if he did, no harm would come to the ship. Then, the story goes, the chief began to prophesy – the ship would fight with the same crew that had taken her to New Zealand; she would be hit, but without casualties. The crew smiled; the ship was due to pay off in September 1914. But war came, re-commissioning was deferred; and although in the thick of the fight the *New Zealand* was almost miraculously preserved.

The picture is pleasing: Captain Halsey in the ship's conning tower at the Battle of Heligoland Bight, 23 August 1914, dressed in the *piu-piu* with the *tiki* tapping against his binoculars as the ship storms into battle, from which she emerges unscathed. The crew's enthusiasm for the amulets was immediate. With Captain Halsey again wearing the *piu-piu*, at the Battle of Dogger Bank on 24 January 1915, the *New Zealand* fought the Germans from 9.30 am until past noon, without a single enemy hit although the ship was repeatedly straddled. On 31 May 1916, under the command of Captain 'Jimmy' Green, RN, (Captain Halsey had been promoted) she fired more rounds than any other British ship and steamed unhurt through falling wreckage as the *Queen Mary* blew up ahead of her. Astern the *Indefatigable* met the same fate. 'Throughout the war,' wrote Halsey, 'on board the *New Zealand* this costume was looked on as a real mascot.'

This is recent history but already doubts have crept in. Authoritative yet confusing is a brass plaque beside a kiwi-feather cloak exhibited at the RNZN Museum, Auckland, claiming this as the endowed garment. When the ship was broken up in 1922, many relics (including the *tiki*) were returned to New Zealand and possibly it was then that someone who had heard a jumbled version of the wartime story assumed that the cloak was the ship's mascot.

For the Centennial Exhibition in 1940, Admiral Halsey loaned the New Zealand Government the *piu-piu* (his personal property), calling it a *maro*, 'a hempen costume like a kilt'. This is certainly the dress which attained such importance for the ship. In his account he neither identifies the donor chief nor refers to the prophecy. So is the prophecy story merely a raconteur's adornment to further improve a good story? Or was it so familiar to Halsey that he did not think it worth repeating? He must have known the story well; and he did not disclaim it.

Commander G. M. Eady, RN (Retd), a midshipman in the *New Zealand* at Jutland, says that although Captain Green wore the *tiki* he merely had the *piu-piu* hanging in the conning tower ready for emergencies. (He was not perhaps of a figure for *piu-pius*.) Admiral David Beatty, who knew of this omission, arrived later to congratulate the ship's company on their performance and their escape: 'I know you all think it was due to this tiki-wiki thing your captain wore, but next time you may not be so lucky, so make sure he puts the whole uniform on.' Finally, not to be overlooked is Admiral Halsey's illuminating note on reaction to the sudden appearance in the conning tower of a captain, RN, wearing a *piu-piu*. It was electric. 'The officers and men who were in the conning tower when I got there before opening fire, were so startled at seeing me in this extraordinary clothing that they appeared to be quite incapable of carrying on with their very important personal duties and I had quickly to explain why I was thus attired...'[28]

'The Most Personal Amulet of All'

Seaman Robert Stainsby, on Captain Cook's first voyage to Tahiti, was perhaps the first Westerner to undergo tattooing, 'the most personal amulet of all', in which the skin is permanently marked by rubbing coloured dyes into punctures pricked with a needle. Stainsby founded an enduring fashion. Even today, as the practice wanes, some sailors feel that tatooing confers special saltiness.

Among seafarers of the nineteenth century tattooing was all but universal. Descriptive lists with every US warship were full of such remarks as 'Goddess of Liberty, r.f.a' (right forearm). With promotion, midshipmen might regret these naïve adornments; sailors too, if they meant to desert. Love emblems, anchors, flags and hearts were ubiquitous. As a token of true love, sailor and girl might carry the same tattoo. On a Danish arm were seen, typically, a naked woman, a sea-serpent, two clasped hands and an octopus embracing a ship. The *Wylo*'s crew were certain that their kindly bachelor Captain H. W. Browne had been crossed in love: was there not an arrow-pierced heart on his left breast? Richard Henry Dana was impressed at Monterey by the smiling good looks and bright eyes of an English sailor on the *Loriette*, in gleaming tarpaulin hat, white ducks, blue jacket, black kerchief; and saw on his chest the words 'Parting Moment', a ship about to sail, a foul anchor and a crucifix. Explaining the latter, Captain Fitch W. Taylor, USN, wrote: 'And so prevalent was . . . refusal of . . . burial to Protestants by Catholic communities, that there is . . . a custom among sailors to have a cross tattooed upon their arms, that if by chance they should die in a Roman Catholic country, their bodies might be respected, and allowed a quiet interment on the shore.'

A recent survey has shown that a certain crucifix tattooed on the back, once widely held to soften the heart of the officer superintending a flogging, is still popular. Rumour held that the lash itself fell more lightly on a picture of Christ. Today, more mundanely, US seamen believe that a handsome display of tattooing protects against venereal diseases.

His name inscribed from thigh to ankle distinguished one ship's boy; and while shipping a Liverpool crew, a master saw one man with an anchor-shank tattooed down the bridge of his nose, flukes upon either nostril. US sailors favoured nudes which brought good luck, but many navy enlistment officers modestly required the addition of a red or blue frock to make the ever-popular 'Miss Liberty'. Sometimes hounds and horsemen gallop gaily down the owner's abdomen after the fox, but find him gone to ground with his tail only protruding from the sailor's posterior! Movement enhances the cheerfully salacious: a girl in a hat, beckoning on a Boston arm, becomes a naked woman with legs apart when the sailor flexes his arm.

Conventional black cats, horseshoes and four-leafed clovers naturally find a place at sea, and the four suit symbols, one to a finger, bring luck with mess-deck cards. Their antipathy to the sea make a pig and cockerel tattooed on the instep or knee a protection against drowning:

> Pig on the knee
> Safety at sea.

A man so marked also carries his own 'ham and eggs' with him and will never go hungry. Once the navigator's indispensable friend, a star tattooed between finger and thumb brings the sailor home.

The anchor, especially the 'foul anchor' familiar in admiralty and naval badges, is an eternally popular choice. In the classical world the anchor symbolised hope and was suitably inscribed with 'Aphrodite our Rescuer' or 'Zeus the Highest'. The idea persisted, but the foul anchor or 'sailor's disgrace' when the cable became wrapped about stock and shank is, in fact, a sad sign of maritime inefficiency and may cause anchors to drag. Presumably the lubberly designer of the first badge, finding a plain anchor dull, added a curling rope for prettier effect.

Ships in Bottles

In the Middle Ages ship-engraved stone amulets were carried as charms against shipwreck; later the ship-motif appeared consistently in wool-pictures, embroidery, 'scrimshaw' work and other sailors' handicrafts. The choice may seem obvious. Yet until this century life afloat was cheerless and, for residents of the forecastle at least, an escapist image might surely have

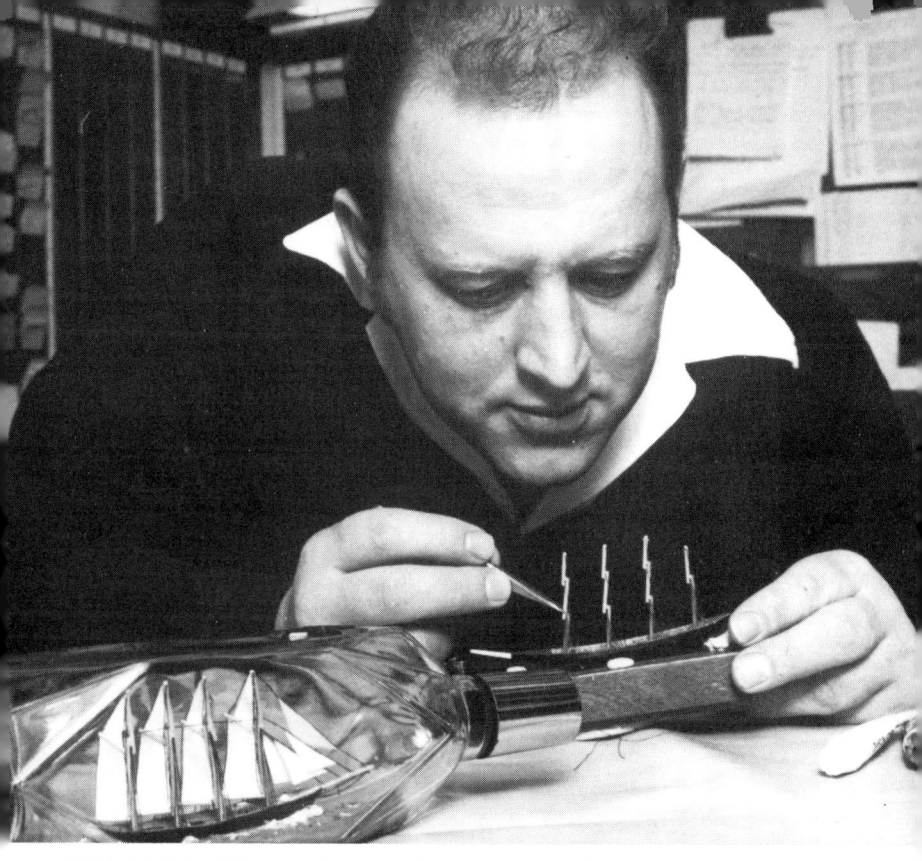

COEMN 'Phil' Filby of the Royal Navy, at work in HMS *Tartar*, putting a ship model into a bottle, a craft traditional with sailors for over 150 years. In earlier years it had strong magical overtones

had greater appeal? One must seek a deeper reason than the sailor's affection for his 'home'. For whatever attractive alternatives offered, the ship herself has always been carefully selected as favourite motif. Rarely, if ever, does she appear storm-racked but rather proceeding swan-like in seas richly blue, white sails filled by fair winds, or at evening anchor in golden harbours. If de Loutherbourgs and van de Veldes were charmed by tempests and tattered ensigns, sailors were not. Portraying disasters merely brought them nearer; selecting tranquil scenes caused them to be. It was creative magic.

Inserting ship models into glass bottles, a lively if no longer magical conceit dating from the early nineteenth century, had similar purpose. Among those still working on the craft in the old tradition is the Royal Navy's COEMN 'Phil' Filby who, while serving in the frigate HMS *Tartar* in Icelandic waters in 1976, 'launched' a gaff-rigged schooner. The ship, a replica of a North American four-masted schooner, masts lying along her hand-carved hull, passed narrowly down the bottle-neck to rest upon a blue foam-flecked sea within. Miniature rigging lines were gently hauled and the masts rose, spars spread out, sails unfurled and billowed. The intentions underlying the enclosing of ships in bottles were not discussed by early makers (and were probably unacknowledged) but they were undoubtedly magical. There was virtue in putting a ship into a protected place where nothing could injure or endanger her. The sailor was in effect 'corking up' fair breezes and blue seas for his own use. Such models, hostages to fortune left with family or friends, ensured the sailor's safe return from a voyage which he had done his best to see would resemble that of the bottled ship, tranquilly proceeding on the parlour chimneypiece.

Animal Mascots

Luck-bringing animal mascots, long valued by ships, must be rescued at all costs if the ship sinks, or the crew's fate is sealed. None must be killed except for food (this cogent argument pardoned one billy-goat on trial for butting the captain). Crews bitterly resented interference with pets; it was tampering with luck itself. One sorely-tried first lieutenant who testily ordered ashore all the ship's pets was confronted the next morning by a donkey tethered to the torpedo tubes by twenty-two yards of the heaviest chain cable. It was freed only after an hour's work by the artificer.

Like rats, cats have foreknowledge of wreck and will leave a doomed ship. Several passengers, including George Gott, noticed the cat of the New England paddle-steamer *Portland* carry her kittens ashore to a warehouse on India Wharf, Boston, just before the ship sailed on 26 November 1898. Mr Gott did not embark, nor did the cat. Others, too, decided that what was not good enough for the cat was not good

Fred Wunpound, ship's cat of HMS *Hecate*, said to be the last ship's cat in the Royal Navy. Fred 'swallowed the anchor' in 1975 and died ashore in 1976. He had two good conduct badges; and one mark of 'disgraceful conduct' following an incident in Brixham fishmarket!

enough for them. It was a wise decision – the ship was lost that night in a hurricane.

The sea-cat, indispensable·in rat-ridden wooden ships, was, like land-cats, of double aspect; lucky certainly but, as befitted a witch's assistant, with an uncanny influence on weather (discussed in a later chapter). Americans permit white cats only on ships; any fisherman meeting a black cat may defer sailing. On British ships one black cat was lucky, two never; but in 1976–8 a tradition of a thousand years was broken when, heeding Britain's strict anti-rabies legislation, both the Royal and Merchant Navies set their ships' pets ashore for good.

One of the traditional luck-bringers was Leading Seacat Fred Wunpound, believed to be the last ship's cat in the Royal Navy. Fred died at his retirement home ashore in 1976. At the age of six weeks he was 'pressed into service' from the Plymouth pound of the RSPCA (a 'bounty' of £1 was paid for him – hence his name) and he afterwards travelled over

Peggy, bulldog mascot of HMS *Iron Duke*, who served at the Battle of Jutland and held three medals. She knew all the bosun's 'calls', enjoyed PT with the ship's company and joined in football matches (on *Iron Duke*'s behalf). She slept in a hammock and when she died in 1923 was buried at sea with full honours

250,000 miles while serving as the much-admired mascot of **HMS** *Hecate*. Noted for his gleaming black coat, Fred, who laid claim to the title of 'world's most travelled cat', lived in a wicker basket next to the ship's gyro-room near her centre of gravity for he never really got his sealegs. 'Missed ship on sailing' (and the warrant issued for his arrest) and his qualifications for 'kit upkeep allowance' did not go unnoticed in his service documents. He received regular promotions until he became Leading Seacat in 1971; and when he 'swallowed the anchor' in 1975 and was 'discharged to shore', he held two good conduct badges, together with one mark against him of 'disgraceful conduct', after an incident in Brixham fishmarket!

For the ship's company of **HMM** *Sandown* (Commander K. M. Greig, RN) a potent source of luck and safety during the dive-bombing and shelling of the Dunkirk evacuation in 1940 was their dachshund mascot, Bombproof Bella, to whose presence on board they ascribed their survival in many tight corners.[29]

Another mascot, Sport, received a moving tribute from Captain H. W. Maynard, master of the US lighthouse tender *Hyacinth*. Sport was 'a sweetwater dog but one with much salt in him' and 'everybody's friend'. He had been pulled from the Milwaukee River in a storm in 1914 and spent twelve years on the *Hyacinth*:

> There was no place on the vessel that he did not visit and nothing going on that he did not have a hand or paw in. He swam and played baseball with the boys, no boat could go ashore without Sport. On 19 July 1926 Sport died of old age; he was sewn in canvas and buried at sea on the following day, two miles off Ludington, Michigan. All hands mustered on the spar deck and a few words were said for Sport to the effect that he had been taken from the waters and was now being returned to them; he was slid off the gangplank by a bunch of solemn-looking boys. He was given a salute and thus ended Sport, the best dog I have ever known.[30]

There have even been sea-going skunks. Flower belonged to Lieutenant Richard Thompson of the US nuclear submarine *Seadragon* and only an objection from the medical authorities prevented her voyaging under the North Pole as the first true 'Pole cat'. In 1964 the adventures of Alphonse, skunk mascot of HMS *Saintes*, were told by Lieutenant-Commander David Gunn in *Alphonse – The Seafaring Skunk*. The author and Alphonse were photographed in the Mall but the skunk escaped and, when caught, ungratefully bit his owner's finger to the bone. At a London hospital Lieutenant-Commander Gunn explained his injury as, 'Just bitten by a skunk in the Mall'. 'And I'm the Queen of Sheba,' replied the receptionist.

Animal mascots are not necessarily alive. Alec Rose was accompanied by Algy, a large, white, toy rabbit. At the Line they both toasted Father Neptune and invited him on board – although Algy, who hated getting his feet wet, was afraid of being ducked. At the very end of the voyage, as *Lively Lady* made fast to a buoy off Southsea beach, Algy came on deck to wave to the crowd of 250,000 who gathered to welcome the yacht home.

'Friday Sail, Friday Fail'

Certain days are tabooed at sea. Sailors still dislike starting voyages on Fridays ('Friday sail, Friday fail'), a shadowed unhappy day of fast and penance with confused traditions. On that day are supposed to have occurred the Temptation and Banishment from the Garden of Eden, the Flood, and the Crucifixion. Fishermen dislike working a new boat or moving to new fishing grounds on Fridays and, in the past, few shipping companies contemplated dispatching a passenger vessel then (any more than they offered 'Cabin No 13'). Only the foolhardy ended a voyage on Friday; this merely stored up trouble for the next trip. But, exceptionally, Spanish sailors favour Fridays, for Columbus began his great voyages then.

There are many stories. Admiral 'Jackie' Fisher, no dreamer, was horrified when Admiral Sturdee announced his intention of clearing Devonport to pursue the German Admiral von Spee on Friday, 13 November 1914. 'Friday the thirteenth – *what* a day to choose!' The date was changed.[31] When the *Olivebank* left Melbourne on a Friday, the crew declared that the Cape Horn weather would be the dirtier for it.

The sailmaker recorded all the *Peking*'s voyages, underscoring the ill-starred in red. A Friday start in 1911 ended in shipwreck; another in 1924 in a broken rudder and stranding. Each time half the crew was lost. In 1929 she cleared Hamburg for Chile on a Friday and mindful of superstition her captain anchored overnight in the River Elbe; to 'vale' down river on Friday was just permissible, but the *sea* must be reserved for Saturday. Closed until Saturday too was the ship's log. But such stratagems were not reliable said the sailmaker: 'On Friday we left port . . . whether that was in the log or not makes no difference. I have had experience: we'll be shipwrecked; we'll never get back to Hamburg.' Nothing so drastic occurred although later foul weather convinced the crew that Neptune had not been fooled.[32]

Captain Frederick Marryat, RN, (1792–1848) noted the view of 'one of our most gallant admirals', the friend of Nelson: 'Why, I was once fool enough to believe that it was all nonsense, and I did one cruise, sail on a Friday, much to the annoyance of the men. The consequence was that I run my ship aground, and nearly lost her . . . nothing shall induce me to sail on a Friday again!'[33]

Although actual fishing was forbidden, Swedes set nets at Christmas for luck; Greek fishermen of Tarpon Springs, Florida, still lie up in port over the Twelve Days of Christmas; and fishermen of Scotland's east coast rarely sailed on New Year's Day until blood had been drawn – and would pick a quarrel to make it so! If they fished at Candlemas or on Easter Day Bretons lost mackerel to porpoises. Easter fishing is still shunned and a number of Newfoundland trawlers refused to fish on Easter Day 1976, when ordered to do so by owners. Good Friday fishing produced alarming hauls of crosses, said Bretons; and from the Baltic to France all avoided All Hallows'

Eve and All Saints' Day, feasts of the dead, when crews were accompanied by shadowy doubles, nets trawled up skeletons and winding sheets, and drowned voices were heard in the wind.

The first Monday in April, Cain's birthday and the day of Abel's death; the second Monday in August, when Sodom and Gomorrah were destroyed; and 31 December when Judas killed himself, were ill-fated days to begin a voyage. It was wisest to sail at the moon's decrease; tides, and by inference high seas, grew with the moon. To be third vessel in line leaving harbour is still unlucky and ingenious Ulstermen may still lash leading boats together and pass them through as one, to confound malignant spirits.

Seamen's Goods

To perforate the psychic entity of a ship's security is as dangerous in the eyes of sailors as piercing her hull. To lose overboard bucket, broom or swab destroys wholeness, and suggests that sailors may follow. Ship-to-ship loans are still discouraged, for such acts disperse good luck, but if loans *are* made the article must be damaged a little beforehand, and thus fortune remains with the owner. Theft likewise 'steals away the luck' and some skippers will pay ridiculous prices to recover lost equipment. In the fishing villages round Finistère, purification follows theft.

Old sailors saw sinister import in carelessness. A hatch upturned on deck, a chart reversed, such things invite the vessel to follow suit. Magically, simulation creates events. A perplexing element in the mystery of the *Mary Celeste* (found in good order, yet abandoned, in the Atlantic in 1873) was an upturned hatch on deck, something no seasoned sailor permitted; and while no one said that this had caused the calamity, some undoubtedly thought it. Similarly the Chinese dislike shoes on deck, soles uppermost; West Indians, a calabash gourd; a Scottish skipper confronted by an upturned washbowl would not sail at all (an aversion exploited by indolent deck-boys). Flowers, suggesting wreaths and death, are unwelcome on board, a belief particularly strong among early submariners – in danger as much from their boats as from the enemy.

Black suitcases or holdalls are shunned, presumably because they suggest coffins in shape and colour. Only blunt knives are permitted at sea – adequate for cutting rope or wood, unlikely to rip sails and useless for stabbing a shipmate in a fight. Ashore and afloat colours are bound up with luck. Sailors shunned white-handled knives as vigorously as they did white stones in ballast. But as usual US taboos reverse; many fishermen there insist on pure white woollen mittens and the ever-popular white-toed 'work socks' ensure that their wearer will never be tripped by the 'little folk'.

A broom displayed at the masthead carries a variety of possible messages: that a ship is for sale; that a change of ownership is imminent; that a fresh wind is sought. Legend relates that the Dutch Admiral Marten Harpertszoon Tromp (1597–1653) in 1652, to show that he would 'sweep the English from the seas', lashed a broom to his mast when he met Cromwell's fleet. But was the act (disputed as 'out of character' by the Dutch) perhaps misunderstood? Tradition long held that an old broom tossed overboard produced a required breeze. Was Tromp's broom a jocular charm to bring him to the enemy? Or perhaps a triumph song for the capture of English ships off Dungeness? Between the wars the US Navy winners of battle efficiency and gunnery competitions traditionally hoisted new corn-brooms in token of victory. The famous submarine *Wahoo* (Lieutenant-Commander 'Mush' Morton, USN) entered Pearl Harbor after a triumphant patrol against the Japanese in World War II wearing this ancient token of supremacy; and at the close of both world wars, ships of the Royal Navy mastheaded brooms to proclaim that the seas had been swept clear of a formidable foe.[34]

Jonahs

Jonah's biblical misfortunes are notorious. On passage from Joppa in a storm, suspicion lighted on him as progenitor of the ship's calamities, he was cast overboard and the sea calmed. 'Jonah' came to describe any man or animal whose presence brought ill-fortune to a ship.

Those uneasy shipmates the 'Russian Finns', whose weather powers are described in Chapter 7, were natural Jonahs. It paid to be polite to such awkward enemies who 'ill-wished at pleasure'. 'I've been plaguey civil to that man all the voyage,' declared a ship's cook of a member of the celebrated tribe, whose enviable gifts included second sight, the ability to talk to seagulls and to draw all the fresh water they fancied from the scuttlebutt merely by turning their hats about three times. Once drawn the water instantly turned to rum!

Those who avoided paying for shoreside entertainment were Jonahs. In 1913 Captain Beckett's ship, coming home from Vigo, hit a Biscay gale which seemed bent on depriving the 'young gentlemen' of their time-honoured gunroom singsong as the ship rounded Ushant. Water lapped at the coamings; the piano would not remain upright. Lots identified the Assistant Clerk as Jonah, he was tried by 'court martial', given half a dozen with a dirk scabbard and by eight o'clock, in miraculously quietened seas, the concert was under way.

Exorcism was nothing if not thorough. On the *President* in 1810, sailing from Charleston, a sailor announced unctuously that *his* sins had provoked the storm – and cast himself over the side. When another gale blew up the crew cried, 'Sam's chest must go too'. It did, and the blow ceased. Outside New York a third storm struck and ransacked quarters revealed a single shoe of Sam's remaining; this too flew overboard and the crew sat back, satisfied that Jonah had been well and truly laid.

Captain Jairus Allen of Cape Cod, at sea for fifty years, lost but one ship, a misfortune blamed by sailors on a feline Jonah. The ship was driven on to Long Island in an April snowstorm.

Happily every man was taken off, but the ship's white cat was missing. Next morning the men rowed out to the wreck, ringed by boiling surf; only the topmast and a hammock-like rag of sail showed above water, and in this, peacefully asleep, lay the white cat. The hoodoo (so designated), renamed *Miss Church* after the lost vessel, was presented to the coastguard's wife. The crew, thankful to be rid of her, remained staunchly convinced that the cat had caused the wreck.[35]

Parsons, Pigs and Playing-Cards

Priests are unwelcome on board ship; even the words 'parson' and 'priest' are avoided in favour of 'gentleman in black', 'the upstander', or 'man in the white collar'; and 'church' and 'chapel' by some term such as 'holy house'. If passage by a parson is unavoidable, seamen in the north of Scotland and the islands take care to wash their boats out well afterwards.

In *My Life at Sea* (1912), Second Mate W. C. Crutchley of the *Omba* told of a clergyman, his wife and child, embarked at Shanghai: 'In the first part of the trip . . . all had gone well, no one concerned themselves about the proverbial ill-luck which attends the carriage of parsons by sea . . . it now seemed to have improved by keeping.' Near St Helena a three weeks' calm frayed all nerves:

> It had been the custom of the skipper to make up a dummy whist party with the parson and his wife, but this was now discontinued, and the old man's text as he tramped the poop was loudly spoken and often: 'Oh, if the Lord will only forgive me this once for carrying a parson, I'll never do it any more!' . . . whether it was owing to the foregoing incantation I do not know, but we did eventually get away from the Line . . .

Calamities have been freely laid at the door of men of the cloth. During the second attack on Ostend in World War I, one of the wounded, laid in the forecastle of HMS *Warwick* for greater safety, was heard to murmur resignedly, as the ship struck a mine: 'That's what comes of shipping a parson – admiral ought to have known better!' A naval padre, the Reverend C. Peshall, was on board.[36]

How should one account for the dislike? Is it the parson's funereal clothing and his links with death and burial that make him dangerous? Does his celibacy (if Catholic) hinder boats dependent on the increase of fish? (Nuns and old maids make bodeful neighbours for fishing skippers; and the Portuguese will never store lottery tickets near the household crucifix.) Most probably early sailors, prudently embracing Christianity ashore and paganism afloat, believed that the appearance of a professional rival merely inflamed the sea-gods into dangerous contests of power.

Other widespread taboos at sea are umbrellas, and playing-cards – always strangely connected, as the 'devil's picture-books' with necromancy and fortune-telling. Many skippers stand ready to toss them overboard at the first hint of 'trouble': although at one time it was believed that the deliberate sacrifice of a pack, torn up and thrown overboard, would produce a beneficial change in wind.

The word 'pig', stubbornly taboo from the West Indies to the Hebrides, is replaced by 'Curly-tail', 'Mr Dennis', 'Gruff' (said like a grunt), 'Little Fellah', the 'Grecian', or 'Turf-Rooter'. On Lindisfarne a pig is 'article'; in Guernsey 'avers' or 'possessions'; in Caithness 'cauld iron beastie', for if the dreaded word slipped out in conversation the Scots touched 'cold iron', the most ancient protection against enchantment.

About 1850 a visiting clergyman preaching at St Monance, Fife, unaware of the taboo, chose for his text the story of the prodigal son and duly read the words 'and he sent him into his fields to feed swine'. There was a wave of bowing towards the nailheads of the pews and a great mutter of 'touch cauld iron'. The minister took this to be an original 'amen' and continued, 'to feed swine . . .'. Another whisper of 'touch cauld iron' and more bowing followed. With some annoyance he continued, '. . . the husks that the swine did eat'. This was too much. With a parting bellow of 'touch cauld iron' the congregation bounded helter-skelter from the church and did not come back.

A skipper who met a harbourside hog rarely went fishing that tide and to this day pork and bacon are noticeably less popular foods on Yorkshire and Scottish coasts than elsewhere in Britain. Gales are brought by the very name of *pig*, with the 'devil's mark' on its forefeet, totem beast of the Earth Mother who controlled the four cardinal winds, and able with excited prescience to 'see the wind coming'. On the last grain race on 23 June 1949, the clipper *Passat* hit a 'pig storm' when the first store pig was killed on board, and the captain, rightly anticipating the worst as a judgement for his liking pork, arranged for three men to be ready to hang on to the wildly bucking wheel. They were needed.

'Rabbit', 'fox', 'weasel', 'hare' and 'salmon' are equally and bafflingly forbidden. Indeed the prime insult once yelled by urchins after Scottish fishwives was 'There's a hare's foot i' yer creel' which was guaranteed to arouse gratifying fury. A dead hare tossed into a boat confined it to harbour for the day. The popular role of these creatures as disguises for witches may underlie the prohibition. A visitor to a Buckie drifter, asked if he fished for sport in the district, unthinkingly replied, 'Yes, plenty of . . .' but before he could utter the terrible word 'salmon', the skipper pushed an anxious fist in front of his mouth saying, 'Na, na. Ye dinna say yon word! I ken vat fish ye mean'. The names 'red fish', 'gentleman' or 'beastie' are common substitute names but there is much room for confusion: 'Rabbit's Island' at the entrance to the Kyle of Tongue is better known as 'Gentleman's Island'!

Women at Sea

'Enough to make old shellbacks shift in Davy Jones,' said one, contemplating the thousands of merchant navy wives at sea with their husbands today. There are female officers, even female captains (especially from eastern Europe) and the US

Navy sends its women members to sea. But all this is recent. Women have long been considered unlucky afloat (despite their inevitable presence among passengers: sailors had to put up with that). A priest and a woman *together* on the passenger list was worst of all. Ship-owners were never above fomenting such superstitions; a skipper's willingness to pile on sail and to take profitable risks might well depend upon an absence of females. The taboo faded so recently that when Princess Anne visited a North Sea gas rig in 1969, the press could comment that 'no woman had hitherto been allowed on a rig because of the superstition that ill-luck would follow'. A pregnant woman with her promising aura of continuing life was the exception – she brought good fortune and most emphatically so if she gave birth to a boy on the first night out. A ship thus favoured would never sink and the newcomer would benefit too: he born at sea will have second sight.

Nova Scotian sailors dislike wearing women's hats at sea (Canadian winter woollen hats are 'unisex') and when in 1977 amateur fishermen turned up at Drum Head wearing hats borrowed from wives their escorts delayed departure to fetch 'proper men's hats' for them. Fishermen never allow a woman to walk over or to touch their nets or they will catch nothing. The knowledgeable woman, especially if red-haired or cross-eyed, keeps right away. And still general is the belief that a menstruating woman, afflicted by the 'curse', will injure everything she touches. She must never, for example, sew on a sailor's badges.

Craft and Catch: Fishermen's Beliefs

Some superstitions are common to all seafarers; others concern a select group. In the fishing community, rich in individual beliefs, if catches were poor witchcraft was suspected. York-shiremen held in the fire a sheep's heart stuck with pins and as it singed the spell's perpetrator, suffering excruciating pain, would desist from her mischief among the boats. In Dorset a pin-pierced mackerel, stowed in a boat's stern-locker where nets were kept, 'pricked' any loitering *sorcière* who soon took her leave. (Sometimes sailors, suspecting a foul wind, pricked their sails to injure the landbound witch causing their trouble.) Belgian fishermen shouting '*Le diable à bord*' burned straw in their hold, stamped it out and threw it overboard – stifled by smoke, devoured by flames, beaten to death and drowned, the evil spirit or *bosch* gave up. Every sea-going nation had its own remedies: Japanese boats, for instance, burned feathers on deck and every crew included men skilled in 'dancing away the *bonze*'.

As befitted a substance itself incorruptible and preventing corruption, salt, loathed by witches, protected stable, kitchen and boat. Many fishermen carried a pocketful and many believed that a witch must count every grain in a man's hand before harming him. Some threw salt into the sea or 'salted the nets' before the season's start. In Scotland salt was a substance for reverence – and silence. When in 1905 an Eyemouth boat ran short of salt in the North Sea she hailed a Yarmouth boat with the elliptical request, 'We need something that we dinna want tae speak about'. The English skipper, who knew the drill, shouted cheerfully back. 'Is it *salt* ye want?' It was handed over; but the Norfolkman noticed that the remainder of the Scottish crew vanished below rather than hear the dread commodity discussed.

From the Orkneys to China, casual spitting in the sea is taboo. So vital a secretion, employed in Mediterranean and Eastern countries against the evil-eye, is not to be degraded. Spitting might in any case be ill-received by Neptune. And fishermen, however liberal as to language, never curse their gear or nets, the core of their craft; such behaviour invites failure and accident.

For luck and 'because fish like its smell' Normandy fishermen nail a bottle of brandy beneath a plank in the boat's stern – perhaps in economical sacrifice to fishy gods. Further south Bretons take a swig of brandy, *boire la goutte*, before sailing; elsewhere on Channel grounds gin is the lucky drink – always carried in the same old battered bottle.

Decorated ships taking part in the 300-year-old annual 'Blessing of the Fleet' for 'abundant catches, safe voyages and peaceful harbours', during the Biloxi Shrimp Festival, Mississippi. Hundreds of decorated ships take part

In a custom rooted in pagan salutes, and today a tourist attraction in many fishing communities, fishing boats are blessed at the start of the season.

Coral fishermen of Capri celebrate the Madonna di Carmela before departure each spring. Blessing continues in a number of English villages, including Whitby and Brixham; and at Norham, Northumberland, just before midnight on 14 February, the vicar blesses the salmon fishing with the ancient prayer:

> God keep our nets from snag and break
> For every man a goodly take . . .

In the Etretat ceremony the priest traced a cross upon the sea with his silver staff declaring, 'In the name of the Father . . . I bestow my blessing upon the sea. Under the protection of the divine Mary, I place our boats and those who man them, our nets, our rigging and our sails.' The fate of those scorning benediction was dauntingly outlined ('all boats unblessed are steered by the Devil'). Father Dolhanty of Main-à-Dieu, Nova Scotia, tells a lighter tale: 'I bless the boats at the beginning of every lobster season, on May 15. One year the fishing wasn't very good and an oldtimer said to me, "Good heavens, Father, what did you use last month to bless the fleet? Vinegar? It sure mustn't have been holy water!"'

Seasonal first fruits are cherished. Many throw back the first fish caught 'for luck', once as a sacrifice. The first to carry a catch of sardines to Finistère was decked with flowers – and the first sample landed is still *le bouquet*. The magical cuckoo, partial to skate, merits a sacrificial fish tossed to it by the first boat to hear its cry in spring. At St Malo the man to catch the first fish wins a bottle of wine: he drinks half and throws the rest into the sea. A gold coin thrust into a cork float makes a thrifty fertility charm for American fishermen; another (which caused tremendous rows) required that a Breton skipper's wife sleep with a member of the crew on the night before the season opened. There were ceremonies for season's end; until at least 1800, as a thank-offering to the fish-gods, the oldest man in a Hebridean boat bowed to his sheep victim, beheaded it and allowed its blood to flow into the sea.

Boat-cleaning has special connotations. No boat fully cleaned of scales before the week's end enjoys good catches, for fish, encouraged by fishy smells, avoid the well-scrubbed – a comforting philosophy for the lazy. No fisherman cares to mention that he has a fish on his line, or a full net; for sound magical reasons no catch is sold in entirety – lest it introduce 'emptiness' – for a few fish lying about convey continuity. And the visiting tourist's innocent enquiry as to the size of catches is likely to receive a curt reply; by the doctrine of imitative magic, publicly to describe a haul risks its loss.

5 Customs: Naval and Otherwise

Firsts and Footings

Greenhorns on board could expect teasing. Newly-arrived midshipmen in the British Navy were made to sing a christening parody of Hymn 164:

> Before Thy throne we sinners bend
> To us Thy quickening power extend,

and as 'power' was supplied by a dirk scabbard and the novitiate gulped a glass of seawater, a plate of ship's biscuits crashed about his ears. On windships the neophyte was sent aloft 'to gather gooseberries' or 'eggs from the crowsnest'; to the main-chains 'to hear the dogfish bark'; 'to watch for the Equator'; 'to beg the boatswain for elbowgrease' (he, being warned, supplied soft soap); 'to ask the sextant for a prayer'; 'to find the deadman or the Flemish horses' (rope-ends and foot ropes). Cadet John Masefield on the *Conway* trustingly asking the carpenter for 'the key of the keelson' (as instructed) and was cautioned not to put his foot 'through the garboard strake' – the ship's bottom. Only when the newcomer had vainly wrestled with the conundrum

> The wind was West and West steered we
> The wind was aft. How could that be?

was he enlightened. 'West had the helm.' It was cheerful fun; on the *Constellation* 'the men were fond as the "reefers" of "running" each other, and imposing on the credulity of landsmen'. The short reefer-jacket of the midshipman provided a useful name.

A chalk circle drawn swiftly round the feet of visitors to the stokehold or forecastle by firemen or sailors produced a liquid or cash reward – a 'footing' – and gave the passenger the 'freedom of the ship'. Captain's Clerk E. G. Wines, USN, wrote of the 'footings' on the *Constellation*, 1829–31:

> On the twenty-first of August (1829) I went for the first time to the main top-gallant masthead – to me a dizzy height . . . the old tars laughed heartily at my timidity. I asked them if they were never afraid. 'Afraid!' they replied, 'what good would it do to be afraid? Mr Wines, have you never been in a top before?' 'No.' 'Then you must pay for your footing,' was the next thing. Paying for your footing is treating all hands to a glass of grog on your first visit to a top. This they never fail to demand . . .[37]

'We'll Bury Him Deep . . .'

Once, sailors received advance wages to buy gear and their first, dourly unprofitable weeks at sea were 'working', 'paying-off' or 'flogging a dead horse'. This depressing interlude passed, a pleasanter phrase of the voyage began – with pay again accumulating on the ship's books – and a canvas and wood 'horse' was ceremonially 'buried'. One exchange marking the moment went thus:

Solo: I think, old man, your horse will die;
Chorus: And they say so. And we hope so.
Solo: And when he's dead we'll tan his hide;
We'll hoist him up at the main yardarm,
And now he's dead, we'll bury him deep . . .

At this the 'horse', set flaring at the yardarm, was cut down and fell into the sea. The ceremony, performed in some merchant vessels into the 1930s, perhaps saw its latest – or its last? – enactment during the Tall Ships Race in 1976, when the crew of the brigantine *Phoenix* cut loose their 'horse' of wood, burlap and baggywrinkle. But it was no more than a gesture; the crew of the *Phoenix* had worked no 'dead horse'.

Christmas at Sea

A. J. Pazolt, purser of the square-rigger *Garthpool*, bound from Belfast to Australia in 1928, left a warming account of Christmas at sea in the roaring forties. At midnight, preceded by a boy with a lantern, Father Christmas called at every cabin with carols and presents. Pazolt was roused by a gift of fine cigars thrust on to his berth. Father Christmas then went forrard with gifts for the crew and 'Christmas peace settled over the dark ship'. Careful shaves, neat ties and white shirts formally honoured Christmas Day and with breakfast – a 'royal meal' of bacon, fresh eggs from the ship's hens, and canned pears – went the distribution of gifts from the captain's wife: an alarm clock for the skipper; good coffee for a connoisseur. Festive yarning, Christmas toasts and a great game of deck quoits occupied the forenoon; then dinner, also celebratory, with soup, tongue, plum duff and brandy sauce (the cook's private consumption of pudding brandy was such that he could hardly stand!), cheese, nuts, sweets, paper-hats and crackers. In the great Southern Ocean, thoughts turned homewards with 'Absent Friends! A Happy Christmas to Them All!' Thus passed Christmas on one of the last voyages ever made to the Antipodes by a British square-rigger.[38]

Struggling round the Cape of Good Hope at Christmas 1897, Captain Slocum wrote: 'On this day *Spray* was trying to stand on her head, and she gave me every reason to believe that she would accomplish the feat before night!' 'For a Christmas box' *Spray* ducked her skipper under water three times while he was reefing the jib. He was delighted by a big

English steamer which signalled 'Wishing you a Merry Christmas' – 'I think the captain was a humorist: his own ship was throwing her propeller out of the water'.

Ships of the Royal Navy, evergreens mastheaded, observe Christmas with a pudding often stirred in the making by the captain's wife and the youngest sailor on board; and, echoing the Middle Ages when prelates and choristers changed roles and the Roman Saturnalia when master waited on man, ranks reverse. Sea Cadet Michael Cotton, embarked at Gibraltar in HMS *Rhyl* for Christmas dinner in 1976, found himself 'captain', and as his first official act fined the real commanding officer, Commander K. G. Lees, one bottle of champagne for being 'improperly dressed' – capless on the flight-deck; and in HMS *Bronington*, commanded by Lieutenant the Prince of Wales, the crew's 1976 Christmas dinner was served by 'captain for the day' Leading Steward Ron Patterson, wearing the royal 'woolly-pully' – the navy's uniform sweater.

Another custom nearly caused an international incident. In World War II Archbishop Damaskinos, tall, black-bearded, in the flowing robes and high hat of the Greek church, arrived on board HMS *Ajax* (Captain J. W. Cuthbert, RN) at Piraeus on Christmas Day, to discuss Greece's future. To everyone's horror the ship's Christmas 'Funny Party' – Coco the Clown, Charlie Chaplin and a hula-hula girl, lights flashing on either nipple – hove into view. Recognising a rival in their trade they howled their applause round the astonished archbishop who, disposed to suspect a mortal insult, was only placated by the interpreter's most strenuous efforts!

In another relic of reversed roles, '. . . the oldest man in the ship, be he admiral or jack-of-the-dust, strikes eight bells at midnight on 31 December,' wrote Lieutenant-Commander Leland P. Lovette, USN, of the departing Old Year and the arriving New. Immediately afterwards the youngest sailor strikes eight bells for the New Year. On US ships the first log entry, by tradition, is in verse. Thus wrote Lieutenant-Commander L. Wells of USS *R. E. Byrd* on 31 December 1976:

We're Byrd, Richard E., DDG Twenty-Three.
Some may ask what our labors are for,
But the two hundredth year, despite some fear,
Saw the nation without any war.

If one's lesson's been learned, it's that freedom is earned.
Our liberty's only on lease,
Through readiness pray that on next New Year's Day,
Another year's seen us at peace.[39]

Birthdays, Cakes and Weddings

A ship is 'in commission' while allocated to particular duties, during which time she flies, by night and by day, her long 'commissioning pendant'. The old and handsome ceremonies of 'commissioning and re-commissioning are milestones in a ship's life. At the quayside the captain reads the commissioning warrant, the ensign and jack are hoisted and the commissioning pendant broken; there are prayers and music and, in the Royal Navy at least, a traditional commissioning cake is cut afterwards with a naval sword by the captain's wife and the youngest member of the ship's company. In 1977 a Texas-style ceremony sent the new US nuclear-guided missile cruiser *Texas* on her way from Norfolk, Virginia, with gifts of a $25,000 silver service from the state, silver from an earlier ship of the name, paintings, medallions, a set of longhorns – Texan symbols – and, up to date as may be, twenty calculators and a set of engraved digital watches!

'Decommissioning' too has its customs. In 1976 the 26-year-old aircraft carrier USS *Oriskany* entered the 'mothball fleet' and on a grey windy day, with her crew of 1,000 on deck in dress blues, she sailed under the Golden Gate Bridge for the last time. 'The 22nd commanding officer of the valiant lady, Captain R. G. Conaughton, instructed the officer of the deck to secure the last watch. The commissioning pennant and national ensign were hauled down.' Into the captain's keeping went the pennant, into the archives went the battered deck log and the *Oriskany* was towed away.

Of importance too are birthdays. In 1976 USS *Constitution*, reputedly the oldest ship afloat, celebrated her 179th birthday with a party in the ship's pierside reception room at Boston, and of course a birthday cake; a year earlier the Royal Yacht *Britannia* celebrated her twenty-first birthday with a cake cut at Portsmouth by Rear-Admiral Richard Trowbridge, Flag Officer, Royal Yachts.

On the wedding-day of a crew-member, Royal Navy custom requires that a leafy garland be hoisted to the masthead. For a seaman this once hung from the mast to which he was quartered in the watchbill; for an officer, from the main topgallant stay. The hooped garland, with fluttering white satin streamers, is then properly laid in the officer's cabin to await his return from his honeymoon; the ribbons are the bride's perquisites.

'Up Spirits'

Rum is the drink of the sea. In 1740, to old-timers' disgust, Admiral Vernon – 'Old Grog' for his grogram boatcloak – introduced watered rum or 'grog' to the Royal Navy, enriching the language with 'groggy' and 'grog-blossom', the fruits of over-indulgence. An old song expressed reverent sentiments:

> For grog is our starboard, our larboard,
> Our mainmast, our mizen, our log,
> At sea, or ashore, or where harbour'd –
> The mariner's compass is *grog*!

The grog issue was picturesque. Every morning the officer of the day and his party, including 'Jimmy Bungs' the cooper, proceeded to the ship's dim, pungently-aromatic spirit-room to collect the allowance, amid odours so telling that newcomers sometimes caused amusement by falling down without having touched a drop! As fiddlers played such traditional airs as 'Nancy Dawson' mess-cooks drew tots for the ship's company from huge wooden casks inscribed in gleaming brass letters 'The Queen – God Bless her'.

But over the years tastes changed. By 1970 the austere living conditions which had made rum a comforting aid to morale had long vanished. Fewer men cared for this rather rich liquor. On 1 August, not without 'mourning' ceremonies, the issue ceased in the Royal Navy; funds saved went to the so-called 'Tot Fund' for Fleet amenities. Exceptional are occasions such as the Silver Jubilee Review of the Fleet in 1977, when the old signal 'Splice the Mainbrace!' – the order ensuring extra rum – was again made. Now sailors must provide their own rum, although ceremony otherwise survives strongly through the use of the beautiful old brass-lettered casks and copper measuring jugs. The origins of the phrase are obscure, but the heavy mainbrace was spliced so infrequently that the words may accentuate the event's rarity; or perhaps hauling on the mainbrace required such effort that a reward followed.

In the United States the Civil War brought earlier changes. Captain Mahan had an anecdote:

> The abolition of the grog ration in 1862 may be looked upon as a chronological farewell to a picturesque past . . . a protest was recorded by one eccentric character . . . who hoisted a whiskey demi-john at the peak of his gun-boat – the ensign's allotted place. To the admiral's immediate demand for an explanation, he replied that that was the flag he served under.[40]

A newly-promoted officer 'wets his stripe' with drinks all round ('Psalm 140, verse 5: "They have set gins for me",' signalled one, thus moving up). At noon, the end of the nautical day, 'the sun being over the yardarm', navigating officers are, or were, on the bridge with sextants, establishing the ship's noon position, and the unofficial signal is 'hoist the gin-pendant' for a 'nooner' or early drink.

'Saturday night at sea', once an unchanging institution with sentimental toasts of 'Sweethearts and wives' (with, from the afflicted, the rider 'May they never meet!') replied to by the youngest present, is sadly faded today. Popular toasts provided:

Monday: Our ships at sea
Tuesday: Our men
Wednesday: Ourselves
Thursday: A bloody war or a sickly season (for quick promotion)
Friday: A willing foe and sea-room (in days of peace 'Hunting and old port')
Saturday: Sweethearts and wives
Sunday: Absent friends

and, favourite of Nelson's young officers:

> The wind that blows
> The ship that goes
> And the lass that loves a sailor!

These were customs of formality. There were plenty of others. So that sailors might indulge in 'sucking the monkey' (a monkey was a small cask for rum) on the eighteenth-century West India station, market women came off with innocent-seeming coconuts – drained of milk and refilled with local rum. The sailors inserted a straw and the resultant drunkenness was long mysterious to the authorities. To make a 'monkey pump' or 'anti-guggler' the thief would insert a quill into the captain's private wine supply, hanging for coolness outside his cabin. Euphemisms glided benevolently over indiscretions. 'Gone to freshen his hawse' described one enjoying a quick after-watch drink; those veering and luffing like a ship almost out of control were 'three sheets in the wind', 'half seas over', 'shaking a cloth in the wind' or, worse, 'over the bay'.

Bells and Babies

The ship's bell divides the sea-day into watches – middle, morning, forenoon, afternoon, first and last dog, and first – of four hours each, with, exceptionally, dog-watches of two hours each, necessary for a diurnal change of watch. On British ships five bells (1830 hours) in the last dog, is replaced by one bell only. Legend relates that five bells in the last dog-watch was the signal awaited by the Nore mutineers on 13 May 1797. The secret leaked out and orders to strike one bell only were given. This practice persists, and is also acknowledged by certain foreign fleets.

A sailor's child, christened on board with the upturned ship's bell acting as extempore font, may receive the ship's name. Many nautical fathers, blinded as to suitability, have eagerly presented the name of one darling to another; a nineteenth-century infant named after Papa's *Boadicea* was unlucky; less so perhaps an acquaintance of the present writer's, indebted with many others to HMS *Hermione*.

Death at Sea

A macabre rite preceded the solemnity of sea-burial. Before commitment the sailmaker sewed the body into its canvas shroud and passed the last securing stitch through the corpse's nose, to ensure that he was truly dead, that his ghost would not walk the ship and that he would remain within his shroud, well-weighted with shot or shackles. An untrammelled corpse showed a distressing predilection for floating and following the ship. He who 'sewed the corpse' received a fee. When HMS *Castor* suffered twenty-three dead in the Battle of Jutland, the officiating rating – who knew his rights – demanded, and received, twenty-three guineas.

Proceedings varied little. About 1845 in a US man-of-war off Batavia, the body of an officer in full-dress uniform was laid within a deal coffin constructed by the ship's carpenter. At the pipe 'All hands to bury the dead!' be-craped officers and crew mustered, arms reversed, and as the band played dirges the flag-draped coffin, on a broad plank, was carried to the gangway. The ship was brought to and, at the chaplain's words 'We now commit this body to the deep . . .' and a salute from the marines, the coffin slipped away. Men's hearts stood ajar at such emotional moments, offering an entry to devils, but gunfire, especially shots to the magic number of three, frightened them away. Then the boatswain piped down; and the ship proceeded. Regrettably, a foremasthand's burial was reported as far less impressive; only humble shipmates escorted the corpse in his hammock shroud to the gangway; only an abbreviated burial service was read and the vessel did not stop.[41]

Captain Basil Hall, RN, left an account of the burial of a much-loved midshipman. It was dark, 'blowing a treble-reefed top-sail breeze', and signal lanterns provided a dim light as the ship's company assembled, on booms, in boats, in main rigging halfway up the cat harpings. Minute by minute the gale rose; the grating on which the corpse rested was almost touched by the foaming peaks of waves roaring past. As the body was committed, 'so violent a squall was sweeping past the ship . . . that no sound was heard of the usual splash, which made the sailors allege that their young favourite never touched the water at all, but was carried at once in the gale to his final resting-place'.

On land, disordered raiment has always intimated mourning, and the same holds good for a ship. Flags are half-masted, rope-ends left trailing, yards 'a-cockbilled' (trimmed to lie at an angle to the deck). In Catholic countries such etiquette is proper to Good Friday and the close of Lent. Once, in the Indian Ocean, a tramp steamer's ensign was observed at half-mast; another signalled 'Anyone dead? Do you require assistance?' and received the hoist 'KRST'. No clue lay in the International Code of Signals; then someone noticed the chartroom calendar – it was Good Friday and the flags spelt 'Christ'. At Santa Barbara, California, Richard Henry Dana wrote of

> . . . the large Genoese which we saw in the same place on the first day of our coming upon the coast . . . a large clumsy ship, and with her topmasts stayed forward and high poop-deck, looked like an old woman with a crippled back . . . on Good Friday she had all her yards a-cockbill . . . some also have an effigy of Judas, which the crew amuse themselves with keelhauling and hanging by the neck from the yardarm.

'A ship cannot abide to be a bier,' say seamen sagaciously. Apparently in deference to hygiene but really because corpses are windraisers and ancient sources of ill-luck, sea-burial takes place without delay. A corpse always rests athwart the ship: 'feet to engines' is anathema to engineers. Crews have mutinied at the prospect of carrying a corpse and an embalmed body in the cargo was always carefully concealed. On manifests, coffins encased in anonymous packing-case deal, appeared as 'natural history specimens'.[42]

When HMS *Colossus*, wrecked in 1798 with a collection of classical marbles, the property of Sir William Hamilton, British ambassador to Naples, was rediscovered off the Scillies in 1976, the belief was recalled. Salvage in 1798 had been sketchy but before the wreck sank, one highly commercial-seeming crate hauled ashore by hopeful islanders was found to contain nothing more than the embalmed body of Admiral Lord Shuldham, who had died in Lisbon. Sir William let fly: 'I have learned that the body of Admiral Shuldham has been saved . . . *damn* his body! It can be of no use but to the worms. My collection would have given information to the most learned!'

Graves of the early drowned are still often to be found between the high and low tidemarks, a conciliatory choice, in the sea's own territory. Certain seafarers may decline to retrieve a corpse from the sea or to assist those drowning lest a replacement for the drowned man be sought by the ocean – and who handier than the interferer? Scott's Bryce the Pedlar expressed a common view: 'To fling a drowning man a plank may be the part of a Christian, but I say, keep hands off him, if ye wad live and thrive, free frae his danger!' Provoking the peril it names, the word 'drowning' is naturally taboo at sea and fatalistic non-swimmers used to make scant effort to learn, regarding swimming as mere prolongation of an inevitable end.

(*Opposite*) King Neptune and his consort Amphitrite arriving to preside over 'Crossing the Line' ceremonies on the battle cruiser HMS *Hood* during her circumnavigation with the Special Service Squadron in 1923

Crossing the Line

'Crossing the Line' invokes images of ocean-liners, zephyred on a sultry Equator, with the time-honoured *opéra bouffe* in progress on deck. Today the prime sea-god Neptunus Rex receives tribute at the Equator; once humbler boundaries also were honoured: Greeks sacrificed at headlands; Vikings at parallels; Phoenicians at the Pillars of Hercules, before entering the Atlantic, 'the Sea of Dark Waters'. Exploration added the tropics of Cancer and Capricorn, the Arctic Circle and the

Equator. When human sacrifice became obsolete, young boys were playfully tossed overboard in token appeasement of which today's merry ducking is a last echo. By the sixteenth century the familiar buffoonery had arrived.

The cruise-liner's 'sacrifice' is in the accomplished hands of the entertainments officer, who arranges a gala dinner on the night of 'crossing the Line' at which passengers often receive certificates 'signed by Neptune' confirming their appointment as shellbacks. (A shellback is a sailor so experienced that seashells are alleged to grow on him.) In the US Navy multiple crossings merit a 'Golden Shellback' award; International Date Line crossings, a 'Golden Dragon'. On a recent training cruise HMS *Intrepid* turned north to the Arctic Circle and the Lofoten Islands 'so that all on board could be awarded their "Blue Nose" certificates'; and when USS *Nautilus* passed under the polar ice she founded the 'Panopo' award – 'Pacific to Atlantic via the North Pole'.[43]

The 'hardest-case' shipmasters, the surliest of mates, gave Neptune a smiling welcome; all felt it dangerous to greet the sea-god's pranks with ill-humour, however antipathetic they might be to ship management. 'To omit courtesies would cause King Neptune to throw the book at us,' said one captain, 'in the shape of storms and illwinds.' In the *Sybil* on 22 March 1780, Admiral Sir Thomas Pasley 'Mustered the Ship's Company to know who had and who had not crossed the Line before . . . stopped a day's allowance from every one who had not done so except those that chose Ducking in preference: at Eleven brought to and Ducked 17 men, who being rather of the dirty race, were much advantaged by the salt Submersion – it obliged them to shift their Linnen . . .'[44]

Proximity to the enemy inhibited no one. On Nelson's 'Long Chase' to the West Indies after the French, Dr Alexander Scott, *Victory*'s chaplain, wrote of 22 May 1805, a blue day at sea, 'The usual Ceremonies on Crossing the Line were performed.'

This was custom: occasionally it was defied. Charles Nordhoff was disappointed of the ceremony in USS *Columbus* in 1845; perhaps a later account by Captain W. R. W. Blakeney, RN, in 1857, reveals why:

> We tried [in the *Acteon*] to observe this custom . . . but as those who had not crossed the Line, outnumbered by three to one those who had, the attempt failed, bringing us to the very edge of mutiny on the high seas. Not infrequently this custom was taken advantage of by some fellow . . . to pay off old scores, and discipline was but barely equal to the occasion. For the objectors in the *Acteon* there was the boatswain's pipe 'Holystone decks!'; it *was* obeyed but only with ominous mutterings. I record this incident lest landsmen should fancy the 'arrival of Neptune' is always a scene of fun and frolic.[45]

Captain George Whitfield painted an equally dark picture. For days his crew pursued macabre preparations; sweepings from pigsty and hencoop were collected; court razors squealed on the grindstone; the 'font' was topped with bilge-water. On the day, kicking cursing victims were dragged forward, and recalcitrants got the worst of coop and sty. Taciturn Neptune snarled 'Whatsyername?' and as his victim spoke, slosh, the whitewash brush struck. Silent gullets were squeezed and received double anointings for good measure. A bloody battle soon raged. Victims attacked court, crowned Neptune (who bore the scar for weeks) with the lather bucket, hammered on with a marlinspike. The captain abruptly closed the ceremony, more to save the barber's life than anything for three victims, faces bleeding from the razor, were holding his head under in the bilge barrel. Captain Whitfield points out that this was really the most brutal horseplay and gives an idea of the type of man at sea in windjammer days. He hastens to say that he is not judging them; their calling, the incredible hardships and dangers which they faced, hardened and brutalised the best of men.

The ceremonies might even imperil the ship herself. Tossed overboard from the wooden battleship *Cumberland*, 'Neptune's coach', a blazing tar-barrel, hung perilously in the deadwater under the counter 'bidding fair to set the ship on fire' until a rare order rang out – 'to tow His Majesty's burning coach clear past the ship'.[46] On the *Norval* a passenger noted that fainthearts bought exemption with whisky; all that is except one jibber who locked himself and his children in his cabin, refusing to emerge – or pay up! 'Cruelty on board a British ship' was the theme of his noisy complaints to the press at Port Chalmers.

Generally, however, discipline and custom were maintained, if frailly. In 1942 the US submarine *Wahoo* dived under the Equator; there appeared Neptune, Amphitrite (elegant in seaweed and rope-yarn), Davy Jones, Scribe, Doctor, Executioner, Chaplain, Navigator and Royal Baby (the fattest man on board, in the buff except for a giant diaper). Neptune wore the captain's old bathrobe and carried a broomhandle with battery-charged tips – to test his victims' 'vitality'. Formidable dough pills of tabasco sauce, chilli powder, iodine, castor oil, vinegar and soap were administered and since for submariners 'bathing' was impossible, oaths and medicals gained in stature. Novitiates, blindfolded and assisted by flailing paddles, approached on their knees to, 'Will you swear to be a faithful, loyal subject' . . . 'I will!' Then, 'Prove it by kissing the Royal Baby's bottom'. Thus were shellbacks made.[47]

Full of a sense of *temps perdu,* of a leisured world not again to be enjoyed, is the account by Instructor-Lieutenant C. R. Benstead, RN, in *Round the World with the Battle-Cruisers,* of Neptune's encounter in 1923 with HMS *Hood.* On board the flagship ('The Mighty Hood') 'Neptune's ripplemaster' made known 'His Oceanic Majesty's' intention of holding court. Rear-Admiral Sir Frederick Laurence Field, KCB, CMG, in command of the Special Service Squadron, flying his flag in the *Hood*, replied: 'For Your Oceanic Majesty King Neptune. Greeting! It is with great satisfaction that I again cross, after many years, the central boundary of Your domain. I look forward with pleasurable anticipation to meeting You and Your Court once more.'

At two bells in the first watch, as an expectant ship's company assembled at every vantage point – the wardroom on the compass platform roof, snotties in mid-air on signal halyards – the lookout's shout was heard, 'Line right ahead, Sir!' followed by the order, 'Stand by to clear away Line!'

The officer commanding the Royal Marines guard drew his sword; bells clanged and *Hood* 'crashed' into the Equator with a flash of crimson fire (a Very pistol was a useful prop). In the tropical night a deep voice boomed: 'Ahoy! What ship?' 'His Britannic Majesty's battle-cruiser *Hood* flying the flag of Vice-Admiral Sir Frederick Field,' replied the captain. 'Where are you from – and whither are you bound?' 'We are from Plymouth and bound for the seven seas embracing King George's mighty Empire! Who are you?' 'I am Neptune, Lord of All the Seas and King of All the Oceans, and I claim to come on board.' And His Majesty continued:

> Admiral, Captain, Officers and Crew,
> Our pleasure's great today in meeting you.
> You are a seagoing race and now or later,
> You, most of you, must cross this 'ere Equator!

Searchlights stabbed the gloom. To much applause Neptune, grasping his trident, appeared 'up the hawsepipe' with golden-haired Amphitrite (a leading telegraphist) at his side, fan in hand, fashionable in hobble-skirt and silk shoes. And behind came a leaping band of barbers, waving razors white and red, doctors, bears (notable for muscular development and unkemptness), pages, port and starboard lights, maids of honour, secretary, cushion-bearer and the bodyguard, fingering their weapons. The Royal Marines came to a crashing salute. 'Simply splendid,' murmured Number One.

At the quarterdeck's afterend stood the throne with, to port, the operating theatre and canvas bearpit, or salt-water bath. In solemn procession, the band playing the 'Battle-Cruiser's Song' (words unpublished), Neptune, his consort and court disposed themselves. The admiral invited the party to 'have one', champagne cup circulated, and Neptune rose to declare:

> Hear the royal utterance from our court
> At latitude which most maps number nought!
> . . . landlubbers yet
> Until our royal certificate ye get!
> We've come aboard tonight to warn you all
> That on the morrow we again shall call.
> And then let those who are not of our order
> Come well prepared to cross the royal border . . .
> 'Tis thus and only thus, that ye shall be
> Enrolled as Neptune's 'True Sons of the Sea' . . .
> At nine tomorrow, when the sun is high,
> Hither again, in state we both shall hie!
> To see the gentle ceremonies due
> Are executed by our retinue.
>
>> Shave him and bash him,
>> Duck him and splash him,
>> Torture and smash him,
>> And don't let him go!

shrieked the bears prophetically, as the condemned retired for the night.

On 15 December, *Hood* steamed leisurely southward over sapphirine seas, and Neptune again appeared:

> Good bathing, loyal subjects! 'Tis our will
> On this auspicious day, by royal decree
> In ancient ceremony to fulfil,
> Namely, to grant the Freedom of the Sea;
> So let all novices and those unversed
> In ozone law, be ready for the worst!

One thousand aspirants awaited baptism. Orders of merit were bestowed early and the captain privately immersed, that he might receive his order with the rest. Long acquainted with the seven seas, Rear-Admiral Field received the 'Order of the Briny Bath'; the Paymaster-Commander, the 'Order of the

Bar of Soap'; the Commissioned Ordnance Officer, 'Lord of the Magic Spanner'; the Principal Medical Officer, the 'Ancient Order of the Grinning Skull'; and the Engineer Commander (already a 'Knight Commander of the Trident') evoked:

> 'Tis water that we rule; with you, 'tis oil
> That helps you wield your mighty power so far.
> Indeed, 'tis part of Our domain you boil,
> So rise! Commander of the Old Fire Bar!

Then from the bath crawled a waterlogged Captain J. K. Im Thurn, OBE, RN, attempting to destroy the taste of soap. He heard:

> We'll grant our royal protection on your trip!
> So rise! Commander of the Old Log Ship!

Final proceedings began. The bears stampeded to the pit. Neptune's police combed the ship for fugitives. An unlucky cook, innocently peeling onions for his captors' dinner, was dragged on deck, stuffed into his own onion sack. ('Found skulking amid the onions? Let the smell be washed from him!') Amid scenes of revolution, 'Jaunty' – the master-at-arms – was welcomed on deck.

Victims were seized by 'doctors', dosed with petrol, castor oil, vinegar and seawater, whitewashed and shaved with Brobdingnagian razors, shoved backwards by bears into the increasingly turbid bath (oakum fur washes off). They emerged, spluttering, to King Neptune's smile and handshake, while his secretary recorded names with a seafowl feather quill. Gradually the stream of applicants dwindled; Neptune, marooned at last and uneasy perhaps for his own welfare, slipped quietly away leaving his court to shift for themselves. By now every shellback was the proud owner of a certificate which read:

Order of the Bath to All Sailors Around the World

. . . Be it therefore understood that the said Vessel and Officers and Crew thereof have entered our Royal Kingdom and have been inspected and passed upon by my Royal Self and also by the officers of my Royal Staff and . . .

Be it known by all ye Landlubbers that —— has been gathered to our fold and from now and ever shall enjoy our Royal Protection . . .

Moreover be it understood that by virtue of the power invested in me by all living things of the Sea, I do hereby command my subjects, such as Mermaids, Sea Serpents, Dolphins, Polliwogs, Whales, Sharks, Eels, and others from eating, playing with or otherwise maltreating his person, should the aforesaid fall overboard.

Disobey these orders under penalty of My Royal Displeasure

Given under my Hand and Seal in my Northern Realms this 82nd day of Octopus 1157 FFT (Flying Fish Time) 1923 AD.

All this happened long ago. 'King George's mighty Empire' and the much-loved *Hood* have passed away, but 'crossing the Line' still lives. In 1976 in HMS *Antrim*, flying the flag of Vice-Admiral A. S. Morton, Flag Officer, First Flotilla, on passage to the Seychelles, 'King Neptune held court on the flight deck . . . amid customary ceremony, many of the ship's company, from the captain downwards, were hurled to the bears in the pool'.

Flags and Salutes

Many flags have changed their meanings over the years but, as a 'general recall' to crews, since at least the late eighteenth century ships about to sail have mastheaded the blue and white 'Blue Peter', letter 'P' in the International Code of Signals (perhaps taking its name from the French *partir*, to depart). During divine service on board, a warship wears the church pendant – the source of at least one signal story. An American destroyer, discovered during World War II flying the 'church pendant' and the 'interrogative' flag, explained that she meant to convey, 'God, where am I?'

The national ensign flown upside down has long been a signal of distress, and, knotted to a mast, an indicator of bankruptcy. Conventionally a ship places her ensign above that of a prize she escorts. A flag – as part of the ship's spiritual armour – must not be torn or fall into the sea, particularly from a parted halyard, and many seamen also avoided repairing a flag on the quarterdeck or handing one through a companion ladder, believing vaguely that such acts brought ill-luck.

When a ship sails home to 'pay off', by a custom in vogue since the Napoleonic wars, from her main-truck streams the narrow white bunting 'paying-off' pendant, once varying in length with the length of her commission. From the masthead of **RMS** *Queen Mary*, on her last Atlantic voyage in 1967 flew 310 nostalgic feet of pendant, ten for every year of service. By virtue of once having supplied the indispensable pig's bladder, gilded and gleaming, which held the 'fly' from the water (a job done today by prosaic rubber balloons), the naval cook is privileged to hoist this much-acclaimed signal. And, in the days of much 'brightwork', another cheerful announcement of homegoing was a great bundle of the ship's polishing rags mastheaded in token of their not being needed again. In the US Navy the pendant was formerly equal in length to a foot for every man on board and was cut up for souvenirs. The captain took the first star, at the hoist, the executive, the second, and so on.

Salutes of all kinds accompany formal life at sea. Originally warships were saluted both by firing guns and striking topsails. In the seventeenth century, gunpowder being expensive, firing restrictions were introduced. Merchantmen settled for striking topsails and, when steam superseded sail, for dipping their ensigns, a salute still in vogue. In traditional courtesies, intricately interwoven with international protocol, warships continue to use gun salutes. The numbers of guns fired, established by tradition and dependant upon the rank of the saluted, are always odd, even numbers having long been regarded as 'unlucky'. To render herself temporarily helpless and incapable of firing a treacherous broadside, the saluting ship used to present her bows to the saluted. From this derived similar inhibitory devices such as 'tossing oars', 'lying on oars', and 'letting the sheets fly' and in modern times 'stopping engines'. Hand salutes, gun salutes, guards of honour, bands, bugle calls, piping the side, manning the rail (formerly the yards), cheering ship and many combinations thereof are among marks of respect used in navies today.

To the landsman nothing speaks more plainly of life on the ocean wave than the squeal of the boatswain's pipe, whistle or 'call', ancient badge of office and honour, described in 1769 as 'of silver or brass, used by the bosun and his mates to summon the sailors to their duty and direct them in different exercises, such as hoisting, heaving, lowering . . . '. Even today, eclipsed by Tannoy and other broadcasting systems, the magical 'call' remains vital to naval ceremonial.

Similar pipes had set pace for Greek and Roman galley oars. Shakespeare described them in *The Tempest*; Samuel Pepys in *Naval Notes*. In the Old Navy, calls paced the day with such picturesque messages as 'rum bosun to your station', 'away picket boat', 'make and mend', 'all hands to dance and skylark' and, last thing at night, 'pipe down', for hands to turn in. With identifying cadences there were calls for every occasion. Among the lesser known, resurrected unexpectedly in World War II, was 'duty shepherd tend your sheep', heard at Jeddah in the Red Sea when Admiral Sir Algernon Willis, flying his flag in HMS *Newcastle*, received a farewell gift from the Arabs of a dozen sheep.

'Piping the side', salutes given by the 'piping party' at the head of the gangway to commanding officers and other privileged persons, dates from a period when safety and dignity demanded that officers be lifted on board ship in a 'bosun's chair'. A rising note, ordering the 'walk away' with the yardarm 'whip', hoisted the visitor on board; the falling note, the 'walk back', lowered him on deck. It is a signal honour: during the United States Bicentennial, at Queen Elizabeth II's express wish, President Gerald Ford was piped aboard the Royal Yacht *Britannia* in a salute normally reserved exclusively for foreign monarchs in uniform. Equally honourable is the Royal Navy custom of piping ashore the body of any man who dies on board.

Finally among picturesque salutes must surely be included one from the United States, now, sadly, seen no more. The anchor watch, lined up and holding six lanterns for admirals, four for captains, two for wardroom officers, would light the way from the head of the gangway to the hatchway leading to the officers' quarters. When electric light arrived the custom necessarily faded, but Admiral W. H. Brownson, who could not bear to part with so charming a tradition, continued the old practice for years, using portable electric lamps.

Homeward Bound – and Farewell

> Call all hands to man the capstan
> See the cable run down clear
> Heave away, and with a will, boys,
> For Old England we will steer!
> Rolling home, rolling home,
> Rolling home across the sea,
> Rolling home to dear old England,
> Rolling home, dear land, to thee!
>
> Many thousand miles behind us,
> Many thousand miles before
> Ancient ocean heaves to waft us,
> To the well-remembered shore,
> Rolling home . . .

are typical verses of a song represented, *mutatis mutandis*, in the repertoires of half the fleets of the world. Gunther Prien, the U-boat commander, remembered that the German merchant service sang:

> Rolling home to my old Hamburg,
> Rolling home, my land, to thee . . .

of which the bosun alone was privileged to sing the opening words. It was a song sung once only on every voyage, as the anchor was weighed and the ship left her last port for home.

Captain Eric Bush, DSO, DSC, RN, recalls that to hear the song on a foreign station was to experience excitement and longing for home; although a journey of perhaps 10,000 miles lay ahead, with the band playing 'Rolling Home' and the paying-off pendant flying, the sailors felt themselves almost there. Much that made such moments poignant has gone; pre-war days on the China and Mediterranean stations; 'big ships' glittering in the burning heat of foreign suns; immaculate Royal Marines bands playing on deck, all have vanished. Submarines, today's capital ships, have no space for music and 'Rolling Home' is rarely, if ever, heard.

In 1976 in a letter to the author, Lieutenant-Colonel Paul Neville, MVO, FRAM, RM, Principal Director of Music, Royal Marines, wrote:

> The tune 'Rolling Home to Dear Old England' was traditionally played by the Royal Marines Band when a ship left its overseas station for the last time at the end of its commission. I can verify this personally, having played in a band that did just that as long ago as 1948! Changes in the size and structure of the Fleet since that time have resulted in an almost total transfer of Royal Marines Bands from ship to shore and the withdrawal of most of the ships large enough to accommodate a band. These days ships do not serve a specific "commission" on a foreign station and for all these reasons the custom has been gradually dropped.[48]

Until the Panama Canal opened in 1914, the Cape Horn route remained firmly in the hands of big sailing-ships and farewell customs were lively until the end on Chile's 'nitrate coast'. On British ships a sailor rode astride the last Union

Jack-spiked bag loaded; and to the mainmast the ship's carpenter hoisted a wooden frame on which red and white lights blazed like the crackling stars of the Southern Cross (every departing ship, regardless of destination, was obliged first to turn south). The homeward-bounder ringingly cheered every ship present and, even if a mile away, the saluted responded. Default brought a concerted fleet-wide never-to-be-forgotten 'groan', a disgrace dragged up for years: 'Oh yes, you were *groaned* at Iquique on such and such a date . . . .' Next morning, with the land breeze, friendly hands weighed the departing anchor, visiting skippers drank up their whisky and shoved off in their own boats, heartily wishing the vessel a 'Happy Voyage', knowing that they too would soon be on their way.[49] American merchantmen used the chanty 'Rio' to raise the anchor when outward bound and 'Shenandoah' to weigh at the last port before home as overhead flew the black 'nighthawk' pendant, proper to the moment.

It was the same in the navy. The lower rigging of a departing American man-of-war was 'crowded with seamen from deck to top, returning roundly the cheers given by all the ships-of-war present, foreign as well as national . . . many have witnessed also the time-honoured ceremony of her crew throwing their hats overboard with the last cheer . . . those of the homeward-bounder became the inheritance of the boatmen of the port . . .'[50] Hats in the sea, voluntarily or otherwise, were good-luck offerings to wind- and battle-gods.

Homeward-bounders dangled a rope-end over the ship's side for 'wives and sweethearts to pull the ship home'. At this happy moment Richard Henry Dana found everyone in diamond humour: 'At each change of the watch, those coming on deck asked those going below "How does she go along?" and got, for answer, the rate, and the customary addition "Aye! and the Boston girls have had hold of the tow-rope all the watch!"' The girls came from London or Liverpool, Newport or Nantucket, Sydney or Singapore:

> And it's haul away, girls, steady and true,
> Dolly and Molly, Polly and Sue,
> Mothers and sisters and sweethearts and all,
> Haul away, all the way, haul away, haul!

sang the crews to rollicking off-watch accompaniments of paper and comb, tin whistle and frying pan!

Traditional too is the farewell vouchsafed an admiral or captain leaving his command. If he is desk-bound his officers may haul him to the railway station in a boat; if afloat he may be rowed ashore by his officers; if transferred by jackstay to another ship, officers man the lines. At Malta in 1954, Admiral of the Fleet Earl Mountbatten, relinquishing his post as C-in-C Allied Forces, Mediterranean, was pulled ashore by an admirals' crew from the American, British, French, Italian, Greek and Turkish navies.

Leaving the *Northampton* in 1881 was a moment altogether too much for the otherwise imperturbable Captain 'Jackie' Fisher. Commander Wilmot Fawkes wrote: 'He regularly gave us the slip. He went ashore asking for a boat to bring him off at 3 pm. We had arranged to pull him aboard the steamer with an officers' crew at about 4 pm. I received a note from the steamer that he hoped we should not be very angry "but human nature is too weak . . ." So instead the *Northampton*'s band played 'Auld Lang Syne' and 'La Berçeuse', Fisher's favourite waltz, as the steamer passed on her way.'[51]

Custom remains strong: when he gave up command of HMS *Bronington* in December 1976, Lieutenant the Prince of Wales was piped ashore, then seized by his officers (in doctors' white tunics), pushed into a wheelchair and 'invalided out' to the cheers of his forty-three-man crew, who ran behind as the prince was trundled down the jetty under a banner inscribed 'Command has aged me!'

6 The Perennial Sea-Serpent

Ocean monsters have long provided the raw material of fo'c's'le yarns. From the start seamen brought home travellers' tales of giant whales or kraken quick to embrace great ships, stories which in the past 200 years have been augmented and overshadowed by public interest in sea-monsters of reptilian aspect. Of these the evidence, provided by level-headed shipmasters, sea-officers, pilots and naturalists, is not easily dismissed. Mysteries remain unresolved.

Expounding a sighting theory still known today, Pliny the Elder (AD 23–79) wrote of large creatures 'mostly to be seen about the solstices' when 'rushing whirlwinds and rain-storms and tempests . . . upturn the seas from their bottoms'. In *Historia Animalium*, Aristotle spoke of sea-serpents capsizing triremes off Libya. Beneath Japan stretched the monstrous length of *Jish-in-uno*, the cod-fish, who for 700 miles was conveniently blamed for all earthquakes and tidal waves; and, clearly deriving from Arabian marvels, was Sinbad the Sailor's *rencontre* with the fabled 'island-fish', on which the unwary might anchor and cook until their host, singed and coming abruptly to life, plunged to the ocean-floor, carrying ship, dinner and diners with him.

A medieval concept of a sea-monster attacking a ship. Two of the crew mistook the creature for an island, landed and began to cook a meal. Then their host came to life!

Maoris feared *Tipua*, lurker in ocean depths; Fijians, the monster clam and giant octopus; Australian aborigines, *Cata Wangel* of vast teeth and eyes, which laid eggs remarkably like beach boulders. Through the Straits of Gibraltar, howling dolefully, to die upon Valencian shores fled a sixteenth-century monster of whose post-mortem Père Fournier recorded wonderingly in *Hydrophie*: 'Its skull was so large that seven men could enter it . . . two dead men were found in its stomach . . . jawbones . . . seventeen feet long . . .'

Krakens, of malign intent yet indeterminate form, figured largely. Sailors did not linger to examine their foes and a much-employed word described a veritable fish-market of menaces: squid, polyp, octopus and many of their tribe.

> Near Breck-hou, in Sark, they show a cave where a devil-fish, a few years since, seized and drowned a lobster fisher . . . it is difficult for those who have not seen it to believe in the existence of the devil-fish. Compared to this creature the ancient hydras are insignificant . . . if terror were the object of its creation, nothing could be more perfect than the devil-fish . . .

wrote Victor Hugo, the novelist, describing another 'kraken'. And Pliny, well acquainted with Mediterranean fishermen who were vociferous about so alarming a subject, added '. . . no

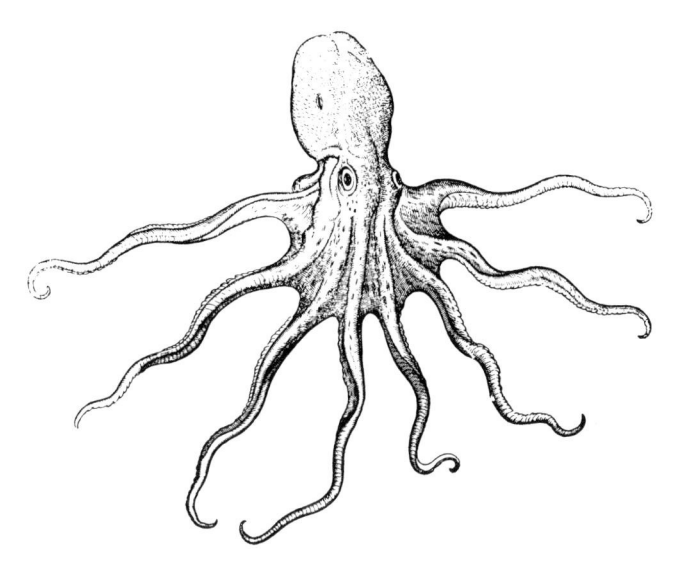

Octopus, often called 'devil-fish' or 'kraken' in early accounts, and the terror of fishermen, who believed that its larger forms embraced whole ships

animal is more savage in causing the death of a man in the water; for it struggles with him by coiling round him and swallows him with its suck-cups and drags him asunder by its multiple suction, when it attacks men that have been shipwrecked . . . '. Fences unavailing, one bold polyp climbed into the fish-tanks at Roman Carteia and stole salted tunny. When finally dispatched by hounds and harpoons its head was found to resemble a 90-gallon cask and 'its beards . . . which . . . one could hardly clasp round with both one's arms, were knotted like clubs, thirty feet long, with suckers . . . like basins holding three gallons, and teeth corresponding . . .'.

Such tales lost little in the telling. No menacing cry, talons or poison, said sailors, yet this creature was most formidably armed. A greyish, undulating shape, thick as a man's thigh, advanced; with eight tentacles the devil-fish sprang at its victim, embracing him so efficiently that it could not be torn away. Mariners named them – in colours from 'yellow' and 'soft earth' to 'violet when irritated' – 'devil-fish' or 'blood-suckers'; scientists, *Cephalopoda*; legend, 'krakens'.

'A Strange Marine Animal'

The classical sea-serpent had its genesis in northern waters. *Jörmundgandr*, the Midgard serpent, strove to bite his own tail as he encircled the world at the sea's bottom, heaving scaly coils to create storms. Olaus Magnus in the *History of the Northern People* (1555) wrote of a sea-serpent emerging nightly from the dark sea-caves of Bergen to devour cattle. The 'Great Norwegian Sea-Serpent' depicts a creature arched above a stricken vessel, snatching a tardy seaman, as others prudently bolt.

A typical eye-witness of the mid-eighteenth century, Hans Egede, a Norwegian missionary, in *A Full and Particular Relation of My Voyage to Greenland* (1734) wrote of 'a sea-monster which raised itself so high . . . that its head reached our maintop . . . long sharp snout . . . blew like a whale, had broad, large flippers . . . covered with a hard skin . . . very wrinkled and uneven . . . it was formed like a snake . . .' Forever associated with the subject (some even proposed *Halysydrus Pontoppidani* for the 'Animal of Stronsa', described later), the scholarly Erik Pontoppidan, Bishop of Bergen (1747–64), investigated the sea-serpent until 'suspicion was removed by full and sufficient evidence from credible and experienced fishermen and sailors in Norway, of which there are hundreds who can testify that they have actually seen it'.

Over the centuries the seas of New England, no less than those of Scandinavia, were resorts of sea-reptiles. As early as 1639 one appeared at Cape Ann; in 1751 Joseph Kent of Marshfield saw another, 'longer and larger than the mainbeam of his 85-ton sloop'. 'In a public armed ship at sunrise' in 1780 Captain George Little met another 50ft long, in Broad Bay, but before his marines could fire 'the serpent dove'; and in 1802, yet another, with 'serpent's head, of a colour as blue as possible . . . black ring round his eye' confronted the Reverend Abraham Cummings in Penobscot Bay.

The first of a lavishly picturesque sequence of sightings astonished inhabitants who viewed 'a strange marine animal' in Gloucester Harbour, Massachusetts, on 10 August 1817. With commendable speed the Linnean Society of New England assembled evidence from among others a shipmaster of probity, Solomon Allen III. He saw a dark brown creature ('I did not discover any spots') from 80 to 90ft long, the thickness of a 'half-barrel', 'joints from his head to his tail' and rattlesnake head, the size of a horse's, and remarked that the serpent moved sluggishly and sank, only to reappear two minutes later, 200 yards away. Eager witnesses stepped forward, including Matthew Gaffney, a ship's carpenter, who pursued the beast 'with a good gun' but with poor aim.

In delectable late summer weather long-headed New Englanders, deep-sea men, stolid as to imagination, at ease with whales, sharks and seaweed, declared the monster to be outside their experience. A snake head, brown colour, and humps which vanished with movement were remarked by all. For two weeks the creature hung about the harbour; snares were unavailing and public disquiet grew. Had the beast laid eggs? In September panic was stimulated by boys at Loblolly Cove who found a knobbly, yard-long creature. Was this the harbinger of the horrid succession? The committee declared the creature an infant sea-serpent, *Scioliophis Atlanticus*, and it was dispatched with a pitchfork. Steadier zoologists identified without difficulty a diseased blacksnake.

For two years reports were scanty. Then in August 1819 at Nahant, further testimonies produced a creature perhaps 100ft long, with the head of a rattlesnake, so close to hand that 'See his *glistening* eye!' was the cry of a 'cloud of witnesses exceeding two hundred'. Two weeks later, near Dallivans Neck, the ship's boat of USS *Science,* carrying the impeccable persons of the Reverend Cheever Felch, Captain William Malbone and Midshipman Blades, spotted a creature 130ft long, dark brown, white under the throat with fourteen 'bunches' down its back. ' "There is your sea-serpent!" . . . a laugh on me, for believing in its existence; but it proved to be no joke,' said Mr Felch. The day made a convert: 'Mr Malbone, till this day, was incredulous.'

Before interest shifted to other seas, in a 'clock-calm' on a summer's day off George's Bank in 1820, passenger Robert Barclay of the *Silas Richards* cried, 'Why, there is a *sea-snake*!' to be assured by Captain Holdridge, '*That* is the sea-serpent. I would give my ship and cargo to catch the monster!' Passengers, grumbling at 'too many hoaxes . . . already' with few exceptions refused to view the wonder. 'I was too eager to stand parleying with them . . .' Looking neither to left nor right the serpent passed 50 yards from the ship: 'We had but one harpoon on board, and the ship's longboat was, for the time being, converted to a cowhouse.' Nothing more could be done.

Daedalus and After

As the century advanced public interest, prepared by such revelations, focussed squarely on the reptilian monster, with island-fish and krakens dismissed as medieval chimera. Sightings, both fore and aft of the *annus mirabilis* of 1848, were enhanced by the arriving age of science. Few captains neglected to mention witnesses, the weather and the state of the sea. Working on its greatest period of hydrography, the Royal Navy, with objective eyes, appraised sea-serpents worldwide; masters of merchantmen were no less vigilant.

Retrospectively such scenes have a hypnotic quality; a calm sea, an attentive group on deck, the lookout's shout, the elevation of glasses, a swift assessment of a dark form, its length canvassed – the sail? the ship's boat? Sometimes a log entry followed but not always for, as Captain Sir David Bone was to remark years later, '. . . no reputable shipmaster is allowed to talk of sea-serpents he has seen'. Some, rightly fearing professional injury, held their tongues.

The most personable of all sea-serpents, distinguished in every body of sea-serpentiana, appeared on 6 August 1848 to HMS *Daedalus*, on passage to England from the East Indies to pay off and between the Cape of Good Hope and St Helena in latitude 24° 44′ S, longitude 9° 22′ E. At five in the after-

An artist's impression of the sea-serpent seen by HMS *Daedalus* on 6 August 1848 between the Cape of Good Hope and St Helena

noon in 'weather dark and cloudy' with 'a long ocean swell from the SW', Midshipman Sartoris suddenly reported 'something very unusual' in the sea to Lieutenant Edgar Drummond, officer of the watch. Unusual indeed, it was a sea-serpent.

The ship reached Plymouth on 4 October. Inevitably someone talked and *The Times* printed a lively tale. Until this point Captain Peter M'Quhae, RN, the *Daedalus*'s commanding officer, desiring further employment and not unreasonably nervous of his admiral's reaction to a story so completely inimical to a steady reputation, had held his peace. Although not absent from private journals the sighting went unlogged, but now, somewhat ruffled, Admiral Sir W. H. Gage, Commander-in-Chief, Devonport, demanded an explanation. M'Quhae's enforced recollections in tranquillity had, as augmentation, Lieutenant Drummond's private notes made on the spot. He drew a memorable picture of an enormous serpent with head and shoulders kept about four feet constantly above the surface of the sea, and

... as nearly as we could approximate by comparing it with the length of what our maintopsail-yard would show in the water, there was at the very least 60 feet of the animal *à fleur d'eau,* no portion of which was, to our perception, used in propelling it through the water, either by vertical or horizontal undulation. It passed rapidly, but so close under our lee quarter, that had it been a man of my acquaintance, I should have easily recognised his features with the naked eye; but did not, either in approaching the ship or after it passed our wake, deviate in the slightest degree from its course to the S.W., which held on at the pace of from 12 to 15 miles per hour, apparently on some determined purpose. The diameter of the serpent was about 15 or 16 inches behind the head, which was without any doubt, that of a snake, and it was never, during the 20 minutes that it continued in sight of our glasses, once below the surface of the water; its colour a dark brown, with yellowish white about the throat. It had no fins, but something like the mane of a horse, or rather a bunch of sea-weed, washed about its back . . .

Hoax, delusion or reality? Some scientists, hot on the trail, recognised a great fossil reptile, others proposed a giant squid, or a sulphur-bottom whale. But Sir Richard Owen, Curator of the Hunterian Museum, argued repressively in *The Times* of 9 November for a seal, such as Anson's sea-lion or *phoca proboscidia* – and no serpent at all! Captain M'Quhae protested understandably that he could distinguish seal from snake. Conflict has long continued over this difficult episode, confusing in all aspects save one, that the *Daedalus* undoubtedly met a living creature of unknown species which was to become the most famous sea-serpent of all time.

Other accounts followed. Captain George Harrington, master of the *Castilian*, in December 1857, in the vicinity of St Helena, recorded:

> ... a huge marine animal ... head ... like a long nun buoy ... diameter ... seven or eight feet in the largest part, with a kind of scroll, or tuft of loose skin, encircling it about two feet from the top ... I am convinced that it belonged to the serpent tribe; it was of a dark colour about the head, and was covered with several white spots. Having a press of canvas on the ship at the time, I was unable to round to without risk ...

Instantly Harrington's veracity (and again that of M'Quhae) was attacked by Captain Frederick Smith of the *Pekin*, whose own 'monstrous' encounter of 28 December 1848 had (perhaps to his disappointment and irascibility) turned out to be seaweed. With alacrity Harrington joined battle: 'Twenty people, including Mrs Harrington and my two officers, saw it as distinctly as I now see the gas light which I am writing by.'

To review every sighting would be tedious and impossible but one of 1872, so colourful as to provoke some derisive laughter, yet chiming with every popular concept of sea-serpentiana, cannot be missed. J. Cobbin of Durban told the *Natal Colonist*:

> During my late passage from London [on the *Silvery Wave*], I saw no less than three sea-serpents, but an account of the last will suffice ... an enormous fan-shaped tail, in shape and proportion like a cobra, its thickest part was behind the head ... head like a bull's in shape, his eyes large and glowing, his ears had circular tips ... and his head was surmounted by a horny crest, which he erected and depressed at pleasure. He swam with great rapidity and lashed the sea into a foam, like breakers dashing over jagged rocks. The sun shone brightly upon him; and with a good glass I saw his overlapping scales open and shut with every arch of his sinuous back coloured like the rainbow.

Respectfully received, on the other hand ('Royal Yachtsmen' are noted for truthfulness), was the *Osborne*'s report of a 'monster' off Sicily in June 1877, with a 'ridge of fins'. Its appearance coincided with the eruption of an undersea volcano, which had supposedly hoisted the creature from its abode.

Still more impressive was a dawn encounter in Port Natal anchorage in 1884: the sleepy crew of the SS *Churchill* descried unaccountable undulations in the water and saw a huge, dripping, seashell-encrusted head of terrifying bearded aspect loom above the bulwarks. Captain Wellington, mounting the poop, was in time to see the animal before it dived. Men, thirty years afloat, gladly testified that 'it was the most marvellous thing they ever saw'. No less remarkable was a conger-like creature with a 7ft jaw observed by Captain R. J. Cringle of the *Umfuli*, off the African coast in 1893.

Scoffers were temporarily quietened by the distinguished testimony of E. G. B. Meade-Waldo and M. J. Nicoll, Fellows of the Zoological Society. When cruising off Brazil in 1905 in the yacht *Valhalla*, they reported a great rubbery, crinkled, seaweed-brown 'frill' sticking up from the water, a turtle-like head, silvery underside and thick neck – 'We were so astonished . . . that we could neither of us speak!'

Wartime and Washed-up

Reluctance to log sightings perhaps pointed to a fear more primitive than that of ridicule. After the armed merchant cruiser *Hilary*, on wartime patrol off Iceland in May 1917, on a brilliant windless day met a marine animal, Captain F. W. Dean, RN, suggested another reason. In *Herbert Strang's Annual 1920* he described the creature as bovine, yet hornless, black, white-striped between the nostrils, and with a flabby dorsal fin. Wartime target practice could not be missed and the unlucky sea-serpent, hit at last, 'produced a furious commotion, like a splashing bather' before vanishing. Three days later the ship was torpedoed and sunk by a U-boat. As survivors were passed up from a dinghy, Captain Dean noticed a small brown handbag which he was told belonged to the officer of the watch on 22 May. Early-trained by a sea-captain of the old school, this officer had passionately begged for the sea-serpent's appearance not to be logged, *'otherwise, we shall never reach port'*. When his request was, not surprisingly, refused, he immediately prepared his valuables for disaster. Captain Dean confessed himself impressed; in thirty-five years at sea he had never before heard of the ill-luck attendant upon sea-serpents, but 'If I ever found myself again at sea in command of a ship and anything of the sort was sighted, I should leave it alone *and make no entry in the log'*.

No sea-serpent has yet been photographed; its bones adorn no museum. Does it exist at all? Many non-believers deny it. Is it a survivor of the sea-reptiles of the mesozoic period, among them the ichthyosaurus, the 'fish-lizard' with a 'ridge of fins', like those viewed by the *Osborne*; or the plesiosaurus, with snake-like head, paddles and smooth body, encased in a supple dark skin, like the *Daedalus*'s animal? If, say apologists, the mesozoic coelacanth, believed extinct for millions of years, could reappear in South African waters in 1938, could there not be other survivors?

Public interest in washed-up 'sea-serpents' has always been great. In 1885 the Reverend Gordon's anchor in the New River Inlet, Florida, was fouled by a decomposing carcass, 42ft long, with every indication of the enaliosauria. Convinced that he had captured the first of an elusive tribe, he 'was obliged to trust its safekeeping to the shore above the tides'; a hurricane intervened, 'the waters of the still-vex'd Bermoothès' envious of their own, recalled the strange waif' and carried out to sea perhaps the strongest evidence yet of saurian survival.

The sceptical recall the maned 53ft-long 'Animal of Stronsa', stranded in the Orkneys in 1808, loudly hailed by triumphant natives as a new genus but easily recognised by London scientists as a basking shark. With acceleration appropriate to the jet age, similar events occurred in July 1976 at

Framboise, Nova Scotia, where a 'dinosaur-like carcass' drifted in. Lifelong seafarers, 'perplexed . . . even frightened', admitted that they 'had never seen anything like it'. But government biologists quickly appraised yet another male basking shark, of all creatures the most likely to be acclaimed sea-serpent.

Public enthusiasm for sea-serpents may be measured by press attention bestowed on a New Zealand enigma in April 1977. Thirty miles off Christchurch, the Japanese *Zuivo Maru* trawled up a decomposing carcass weighing two tons, of an unfamiliarity acknowledged by the experienced Pacific crew who photographed the relic before pushing it overboard. Snake-like, with turtle-body and flippers, it was believed by some to be a plesiosaurus, a claim quickly challenged first by an Australian favouring a mutilated whale or shark, then by a Scot voting for Hooker's sea-lion. Another mystery joined the list.

In every period debunkers seized upon obvious delusions; seaweed, timber, whales, sharks, porpoises, squid, manatees, seals, turtles, oar-fish, even wheeling sea-fowl. Commander C. H. Lightoller, DSC, RN (Retd), wrote of conger eels near the Andaman Islands, big enough to encircle 'a good-sized sailing ship', and in Far Eastern waters sailors have observed huge snakes asleep on the surface of the ocean ('modified sea-serpents!' pronounced Captain Mahan). One 'very thick for its length, of a dark red colour, its scales shining like burnished copper . . . furnished with a fin on its tail . . .' caught the eye of Charles Nordhoff between Java and Borneo. Such creatures grouped, or mating, made promising sea-serpents.

Technology has hindered the quest. Although steamer sightings did occur it was soon agreed that marine engines would prove frightening to large timorous beasts, and with steam came Great Circle sailing. No longer did windships, in tune with the rhythmic movements of marine residents, follow lonely tracks across the sea-serpents' realm, seeking furthering airs. Sea-serpents had early been reported as seeming to watch, even to escort, sailing vessels; now it seems ever less

A Greek vase of the early fifth century BC, showing Odysseus passing the Sirens. They attempted to lure him to destruction with their songs, but Odysseus stopped his crew's ears with beeswax and had himself bound to the mast. His ship passed safely likely that they will again be encountered and such chances grow slimmer every year. If sea-serpents were shy of early steamships, how much more so must they be of today's supertankers.

Comb, Song and Looking-Glass

So much for creatures which may or may not live. Indisputably mythical are mermaids, common in the world's maritime folklore – in Germany as *Meerfrau*, in Denmark as *maremind*, in Ireland as *merrow*. Irishmen accounted mermaids pagans banished by St Patrick; Livonians, Pharoah's children drowned in the Red Sea. The early gods and goddesses in fish form were their ancestors – the Chaldean Oannes; Atergatis, goddess of the Syrians; and the Philistines' 'Dagon . . . sea-monster, upward man, and downward fish'. Pliny had a tale of a 'man of the sea' in the Gulf of Cadiz 'with complete semblance to a being in every part', who boarded ships during the night and gradually caused the side upon which he sat to sink beneath the waves.

At Ker-Ys, Brittany, their traditional home, lived the morgans or sea-fairies, much like mermaids. As sirens, on the dangerous beaches of Finistère they spread treasures of irresistible beauty, only for unblinking human eyes. Fishermen who succumbed to temptation were drawn to their deaths in the waves. Before the prose period of maritime discovery defined her, the mermaid's story (and to the French she is still *la sirène*) became entangled with that of the classical Sirens, who, with women's faces and birds' bodies, feathered and clawed, yet with glorious voices, charmed sailors to destruction. Warned by Circe, the Greek voyager Odysseus escaped their blandishments by stopping his crew's ears with beeswax and lashing himself to the mast.

Time passed. Sailors captured 'mermaids'. In 1560 fishermen caught seven merfolk off Ceylon; these, dissected, were pronounced as having skeletons resembling those of man. A mermaid found floundering at Edam in 1493 was trained as

Portraits published in 1554 of the 'sea-monk' (left) and the 'sea-bishop' (right) fancifully said to resemble monks with hoods and bishops with mitres

a spinner. Early confidence in mermaids was bolstered by the discovery of 'sea-lions', 'sea-elephants' and 'sea-hogs' – with the notion that every land animal had a sea counterpart. Among analogues were the 'sea-bishop' and the 'sea-monk' whose portraits, first published in 1554 by the Frenchman Guillaume Rondelet (1507–66), showed sturgeon-like fish with skin markings imaginatively constructed as features and ecclesiastical accoutrements. The monk-fish had 'a man's face, rude and ungraceful, with a bald, shining head; on the shoulders something like a monk's hood; long winglets, instead of arms; the extremity of body terminated in a tail'. A scaly prelate in dalmatic and mitre, netted in the Baltic in 1531 for the King of Poland, carried a crozier; his assistant was cowled. With the sign of the cross the creatures civilly acknowledged their release into the sea.

But for the susceptible sailor the most alluring sea-dweller remained the mermaid, frequently found singing seductively upon a rock, a creature of other-worldly beauty with long hair (golden, or greener than a salt-wave), silvery fishtail and swelling breasts; a sea-dweller, not averse to 'a run ashore'. Golden combs and round looking-glasses, symbols of vanity, were her accessories. (To her company's delight, the British destroyer *Vanity* chose as her badge a mermaid gazing rapturously at her reflection, with the motto 'If this be *Vanity*, who'd be wise!') Other mermaid effects carelessly discarded on beaches are 'gloves' – *Spongia palmata* – and 'purses' – egg-cases of ray or shark.

Aside from enticement and their distracting presence mermaids were 'weather-breeders' – a sighting of them portended storms – and, as custodians of drowned souls, they were ever eager to increase their stock of prisoners. *Speculum Regali* spoke of a twelfth-century mermaid haunting a deep near Greenland, fish in hand. If she cast it towards a ship, it was certain to sink by tempest; if away the ship would reach port.

The sexual overtones of mermaid sightings need not be stressed. Lonely sailors, denied female society for months, readily succumbed to hallucinations. Columbus reported three on his voyage in 1492; Henry Hudson that in the Arctic Ocean (1607–11) his crew met one, 'from the navel upwards her back and breasts . . . like a woman's . . . her skin very white . . . her tail like . . . a porpoise and speckled like a mackerel'. Captain James Weddell's crew, in Antarctic waters about 1823, met one with green hair. As late as 1947 an eighty-year old Isle of Muck fisherman reported one, comb in hand.

Captain Asa Swift, master of the *Leonidas* bound from New York to Le Havre in 1817, had a full tale:

> . . . at two pm on the larboard quarter . . . saw a strange fish . . . belly . . . all white . . . from the breast upwards a near resemblance to a human being. No one on board ever saw the like fish, before; all believe it to be a Mermaid. The second mate, Mr Stevens, an intelligent young man, told me the face was nearly white, and exactly like that of a human person; that its arms were about half as long as

his, with hands resembling his own; that it stood erect out of the water about two feet, looking at the ship and sails with great earnestness. It would remain in this attitude, close along side, ten or fifteen minutes at a time, and then dive and appear on the other side. It remained around them about six hours. Mr Stevens also stated that its hair was black on the head and exactly resembled a man's; that below the arms, it was a perfect fish in form, and that the whole length from the head to the tail was about five feet.[52]

Captors of mermaids were swiftly disillusioned; ugly faces fell far short of the visions which enhanced art and poetry until the eighteenth century. (Some, making the best of a bad job, went so far as to *eat* the creatures – 'the flesh, resembling pork, served to make highly savoury sausages'.)

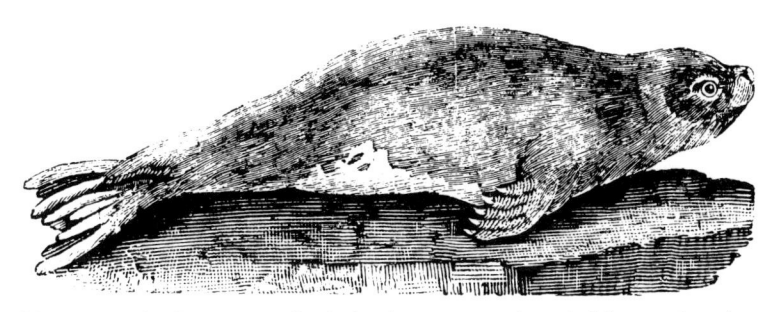

Young seal. Because of their human-seeming habits and cries, credulous sailors have sometimes mistaken them for mermaids

There seemed little doubt that most, if not all, mermaid-sighters were deceived by seals, by dugongs or manatees. These last were perhaps Columbus's 'mermaids' for when the white man reached America manatees thronged Florida's coasts. Folk-myths speak of mermaids' relationship with man. They lived in ocean grottoes of glowing coral and pearl but were curious about land-life and, disguised, were not above visiting fishermen's homes. But should their safeguarding charms – sealskin, red shawl, golden comb, fish-skin or looking-glass – be stolen, mermaids were condemned to land for ever. Lusty stories told of capture and detention by enamoured young fishermen who had laid hands on such valuables.

A Gaelic 'maid of the wave', *ceasg maighdean na tuinne*, rewarded her captor with his dearest wishes in return for her release. Most popular were huge catches for fishermen; unparalleled skills for boat-builders; happy returns for sailors. The detained often settled down as docile housewives and fruitful mothers, but rarely was the landsman's affection returned and the alien snatched any chance to return to her watery home. Should she succeed in escaping she still took a civil interest in her terrestrial descendants, shielding them from storms and guiding them to superior fishing grounds and harbours. Outstanding pilots were descended from mermaids; the entire Irish village of Machaire was thus endowed. Civility was the proper course – an Irishman who killed a mermaid was at once engulfed by an avenging wave and similar waves chased his descendants. Lesser offence caused mermaids to fill harbours with sand. In Cornwall, Sennen harbour suffered thus.

Mermaids smiled on those they fancied and worked woe on the rest. Sailors in a South African port who assisted merfolk to gather herbs received a grateful gift of coral. But human nature spoils a pretty story. When the sailors later tried to net the sea-people they escaped, carrying the coral with them. More happily a Welsh mermaid stranded by the tide on a large rock off Saundersfoot sat with her glass and comb bewailing her plight until a gallant mussel-gatherer carried her to the sea. She returned with a bag of silver and gold. Day after day her protector carried her from the rock; day after day he received his reward, until he was wonderfully rich and the mermaid came no more. Only 'Mermaid's Rock' remained.

At the very threshold of the scientific age some were prepared to view mermaids. One, brought to London by Captain Eades of Boston in 1822, was visited by Sir Everard Home, President of the Royal College of Surgeons, who pronounced a 'palpable imposition' – the cranium of an orang-outang, teeth, jaws and trunk of a baboon, padded breasts and lower body of a large fish. Nevertheless for 'the indulgence of their credulity' nearly 400 persons eagerly paid a daily shilling at the Turf Coffee House, St James's.

Today the mermaid, retired from the sea except as a shipname, beckons on land, on inn-signs, in heraldry, in advertisements – especially for swimwear, as a London theatre name and in church carvings of which the Cornish maid of Zennor is most famous. Appropriate to her eternal siren's role is her garden appearance as a sulphur-yellow single evergreen rose of notable charm and 'when suited, a supreme beauty'.

Foes and Favourites

If mermaids captured a seaman's imagination agreeably, he was brought up short by the shark, his hereditary foe. Nevertheless, sharks and sailors were strangely linked. Primitive peoples told of sharks assuming human form and, in time, taking mates; they might be nothing more than men, bewitched. In the shark temples of the Sandwich Islands priests rubbed their bodies with salt-water to induce scaliness of skin analogous to the gods'. African sharks customarily received sacrificial goats and poultry but in one terrible annual ceremony an unwanted child, chained to a post at low tide, was left until the sea rose and the sharks arrived, when the victim's dying screams were drowned by the noise of drums. Parents believed that the death secured not only the sharks' goodwill, but the child's place in heaven. Response to sharks conceded a reluctant admiration, and their teeth, set in gold, were powerful amulets whose possession invested owners with a touch of 'old John Shark's' own diabolical efficiency.

In sinister escort, sharks followed ships in which a sick man lay. Only if the fish were killed would the patient recover. The flesh of blacks was said to specially delight sharks, although the French naturalist Labat insisted that they relished *white* flesh and, being a good anglophobe, specified that of *Englishmen*. The English naturally recorded the preferred meat as French.

Practised with alacrity by an excited ship's company, shark killing, brutal and bloody, a vengeance for lost shipmates, was – weather permitting – rarely forbidden by captains. The shark's belly was invariably slit open for evidence – such as seaboots, rings or watch-chains – of its last meal. In the *Olivebank* in 1933, the crew's pleasure in a high tea of succulent shark steaks (good if strong) was destroyed by the discovery in one portion of a human thumbnail. Officers and men alike relished the horrid capture, described thus by Captain Basil Hall, RN:

> 'Messenger, run to the cook for a piece of pork,' cried the captain, taking the command with as much glee as if an enemy's cruiser had been in sight. 'Where's your hook, quartermaster?' 'Here, sir, here,' cried the fellow, feeling the point, and declaring it was as sharp as any lady's needle, and in the next instant piercing with it a huge junk of pork, weighing four or five pounds, The hook, which is as large as one's little finger, has a curvature about as large as a man's hand when closed, is six or eight inches in length, while a formidable line furnished with three or four feet of chain attached to the end of the mizen topsail halyard, is now cast into the ship's wake.

The victim seized the bait and was hauled on board to begin its last fight. Its tail became a wind-charm (described in Chapter 7) and the mutilated corpse was retributively slung overboard to the assembled cannibals. Terror of sharks remains lively: the hideous teeth, the threshing tail, the unsleeping hunt for prey, and the daunting aggression as the shark leaps some twenty feet from the sea continue to excite superstitious horror among sailors.

In contrast the dolphin has been the sailor's favourite since classical times. 'Swifter than a bird,' wrote Pliny, '. . . they often fly over a ship's sails . . . lovers of music . . . can be charmed by singing in harmony . . . not afraid of human beings . . . but come to meet vessels at sea and . . . gambol round them, actually trying to race them and passing them even under full sail.'

The Greek harper Arion (c 700 BC), captured by pirates, was condemned to death, but played a final tune, dived into the sea and was borne to land at Taenaros by an admiring dolphin:

> ... a dolphin's arched back,
> Preserv'd Arion from his destin'd wrack
> Secure he sits, and with harmonious strains
> Requites his bearer for his friendly pains.

At Hippo Diarrhytus, a dolphin 'sported among the swimmers and carried them on his back' – a story matched in the 1950s at the holiday resort of Opoponui where a dolphin nicknamed 'Opo' allowed children to ride on her. Most famous of dolphins, Pelorus Jack, lived at Pelorus, New Zealand, from 1888 to 1910; he accompanied ships through the French Pass and was so respected that he received legal protection. His story reflects the distortions which readily attach themselves to legends. Captain Whitfield, repeating harbour gossip, called Jack a '*pilot shark*' who guided ships into Wellington Harbour, receiving salt-pork as his fee. He was said to have been shot by a Swedish captain ignorant of his reputation. Another version, accepting the dolphin identification, states that a ship's propeller killed Pelorus Jack in 1912. Commander Lightoller named Jack as a *porpoise* and, in *Something of Myself*, Rudyard Kipling recalled how his ship had been welcomed by the 'big, white-marked *shark*!'

Kindly dolphins guided human souls to happiness and men to the Fortunate Isles; they were called 'fallen angels' by the Italians and readily symbolised Christ's saving souls. Dolphins meant fortune and safety, and brass castings in dolphin shape were classical naval ornaments, emblems of admiralty and among standard fittings in every navy for admirals' barges. To destroy dolphins might destroy luck itself. In *Lifeboat Number Seven* (1960) Lieutenant-Commander Frank West, RN, tells of the lifeboat's terrible voyage after the sinking of the *Britannia* about 1,200 miles off Brazil during World War II. Overcrowding was appalling; food and water cruelly short. Dolphins, beautiful and hopeful, accompanied the boat on its long journey and, although a suggestion was made that one might be shot for food, Commander West doubted if any sailor present, in whatever extremity, could have brought himself to do it.[53]

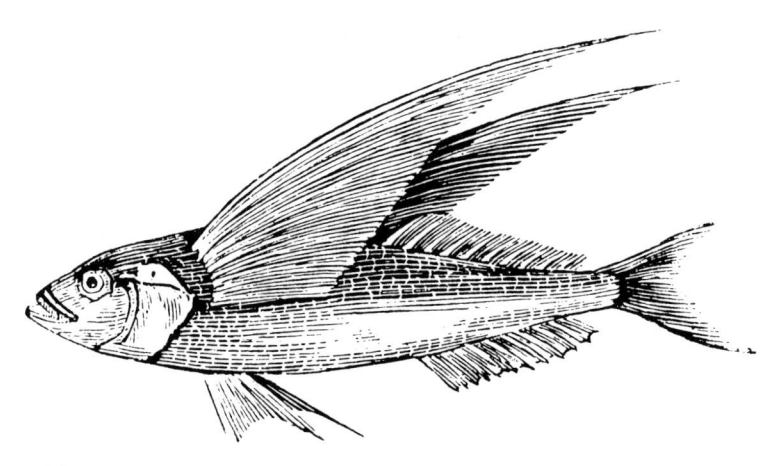

Flying-fish. 'Flying-fish sailors' were members of the élite, the crews of the crack China clippers

Dolphin and porpoise lore is often confused and interchangeable. Commander William K. Anderson, USN, of the submarine *Nautilus*, believed that of certain sights which portended successful voyages porpoises playing about a boat's bow as she left harbour was the most promising: 'No porpoises, no luck.'[54]

Scottish fishermen regarded seals, haunting northern coasts and islands, as women under enchantment, disposed like mermaids to marry ashore. The MacCodrums of the Outer Hebrides were 'descended from a seal-woman'. For this reason and because they embodied drowned souls, there was often a marked reluctance to kill seals and uncanny tales recited the fates of those who did.

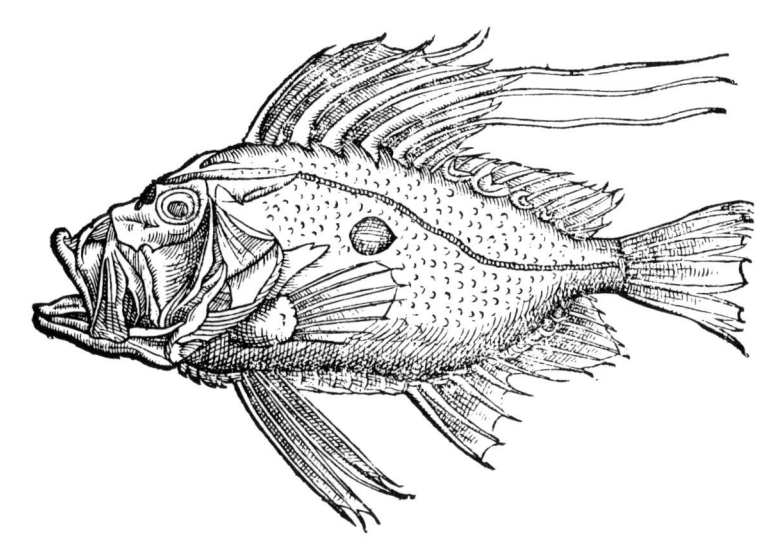

The John Dory, a fish which, like the haddock, bears the fingermarks of St Peter, left by the saint when he withdrew the tribute money from its mouth. It is sometimes called *le poisson de St Pierre*

Fins and Feathers

St Peter, patron of fishermen, left finger- and thumb-prints on the haddock when he took the tribute money from its mouth (Matthew 17, verse 27). It shares with the John Dory (from *jaune dorée*, yellow-gilt, or *janitore*, gatekeeper) the title of *le poisson de St Pierre*. The flounder's side blanched when the Virgin Mary touched it, say Finns; Russians, that the sole revived when the Angel Gabriel had already consumed half of it, hence its shape; Scots, that the salmon's tail has been pointed ever since Loki, spirit of mischief, in salmon disguise was caught by his tail in a net set for him by the gods. To 'eat a holy herring', 'blessed of this world' which vanishes when quarrels are rife, ensures luck. Norman fishermen, uneasy as most at out-of-the-way events, say that the capture of a whiting of rare size signals drowning or accident.

Their prolific egg production has long given fish the reputation of being aphrodisiacs. The Greeks used tunny, sturgeon, scallop and periwinkle, sacred to Aphrodite, goddess of love, whose temples were by the seaside. In Dorset, Poole fishermen complained recently that invasive Russian trawlers had ruined their sex lives. The town, once noted for large families (fourteen was quite usual), has suffered a declining birthrate in the last five years. Said one wife, 'A good feed of sprats does my husband a world of good . . .'. The couple's two children were each born just nine months after the Poole Annual Sprat Supper. In the Isle of Man meals of skate produced large families; of dogfish, male heirs. Water in which mussels have been boiled is still valued in Normandy, and the export of jellied eels, cockles, shrimps and mussels, particularly to the United States and the Far and Middle East, where sexual vitality is highly prized, is a booming industry – called by one happy merchant 'the greatest thing since the double bed!'

Bridging privileges enjoyed by shellbacks include the ability to converse with seagulls, old sailors in new guise; one gravely greeted a particularly distinguished gull as an old Cunard skipper. Seabirds are much respected by sailors. Disaster

A gull must be treated with respect—it might be a drowned shipmate in a new guise. Skippers became albatrosses

follows a gull's death. In New England gulls are the souls of unshriven sailors, flying forever unless their sins are forgiven them.

Commander A. B. Campbell, RD, RN, the celebrated raconteur, told a story from his days as a ship's officer. His ship was carrying New Zealand marksmen to a Monte Carlo competition. In the Australian Bight the bosun came to him in distress, saying that two passengers were taking potshots at gulls at the afterend of the boatdeck. 'By God, I'll stop that,' said Campbell and the captain bellowed, 'How dare you shoot gulls from the deck of my ship!' 'Gulls don't belong to you,' was the insolent reply. The captain yelled back that he would clap in irons any offenders who did not immediately desist. Wisely they climbed down. It was explained that the crew had wasted no time in telling the bosun that they believed the birds to be drowned shipmates and that either the shooting should stop – or there would be mutiny.

The souls of other drowned sailors repose in the noble, half-lucky, half-unlucky albatross, with its wingspan of up to 21 feet, whose fabled territory is the Southern Ocean. Some say the bird embodies skippers only, others specifically that it is that great sailor Odysseus, ever travelling. To permit a snared albatross to walk the deck again was doing an old shipmate a favour. The droppings of this revered bird are still rarely cleaned away but are left for the sea to remove in its own time.

Captain G. C. Dixon, who studied the wandering, royal and white-winged albatross and the smaller birds called by sailors 'mollymawks' or 'Cape hens' from the poop for fifteen years, wrote of the old notion of rebirth in feathers: 'I used to laugh at the idea, but wiser men than I believe that this transmigration of souls is a reality and I have seen so many queer things in knocking round the world that I am not so ready to laugh.'[55]

The albatross may be admired, but it also carries a sinister burden of ill-luck. The *Calpean Star*, bound from South Georgia to Oslo in July 1959, docked at Liverpool with engine trouble after a disastrous voyage blamed on the presence in the cargo of an albatross bound for a German zoo. When the bird died in its cage (some said after eating a sausage roll) fifty superstitious seamen at once struck, demanding their pay at once rather than at the voyage-end. 'I had courage in bringing the damned thing on board!' declared Captain Philip Everett-Price. When in 1960 the *Calpean Star* was reported 'sunk off Montevideo' the superstitious drew their own conclusions.

7 The Weather-Gods

In the days of sail, weather was inseparable from progress, profits and victories. As vividly as on the day when the words were written in 1869, Captain George Moodie's frustration leaps from the log of the *Cutty Sark*: 'Lat. 26° 26′ S, Long. 23° 47′ W. Distance 15 miles. Calm! Calm! Calm!' Another, blunter pen, that of Captain Matthew Ryan of the *Ida M. Clark*, added in chorus: 'Calm! Calm! Calm! Dam! Dam! Dam!'

Every maritime nation accounted for the winds' origins. In Brittany all was still and sailors were forced, laboriously, to row everywhere. One crew, hearing word of a Country of the Winds, pulled their weary way to it and imprisoned the winds in sacks for the skipper to select the foul for drowning and the fair to serve the world. But an inquisitive sailor ripped open a sack prematurely and the evil *sourouas* or sou'wester pounced; the ship was swamped and all drowned. In the confusion the other winds broke free, to the everlasting pain of seamen.

In the Greek story, Aeolus, god of winds, who invented ships' sails, presented Odysseus with a wineskin enclosing all the breezes, secured by a silver string. But again curious rowers untied the fatal knot. The Japanese wind-god carried a great sack of winds on his back; the Chinese 'Earl of Wind, Feng-Po' purveyed breezes from a goatskin bottle. Until late in the nineteenth century sailors were still disposed to call a lively breeze 'a good bagful', and the symbolism of winds persisted long after their assistance was no longer required – the motto of HMS *Hood* was *'Ventis Secundis'*, 'with favourable winds'.

Whistling for the Wind

In an aversion pertaining to aural magic, outmoded, yet surviving, whistling at sea is still discouraged. Such 'devil's music' might goad the gods into dangerous windy retaliation. It was said that whistling in calms produced fair breezes; in a wind, a killing blast. 'Whistle only when the wind is asleep' was the sea-rule. Sir Francis Drake's brilliant seamanship persuaded many that he had supernatural assistance and legend relates that Drake, the Devil and fellow wizards forgathered at Devil's Point, Plymouth, to whistle up tempests and devilry to confound the Spanish Armada. In every country contrary winds are devil's work: 'as busy as a devil in a gale of wind' is a seaman's way of describing one fully occupied. In China a sudden squall is 'Tin-foo-Foong' – 'the devil's headwind'. Naval men, reluctant to honour superstition, preferred to say that whistling might be confused with the orders of the bosun's pipe.

Captain George Whitfield recalled that passengers or mere seamen were rarely entrusted with this dangerous charm, even if, in the doldrums, the skipper on the poop was blowing his own front teeth out. Only the cook was dispensed; he might whistle as he stoned prunes or raisins for 'duff', said shipmates, so that the fruit went into the pudding and not into his 'pouch'. But even naval rules were not ironclad for, 'One might have thought that the ship was planted in a grove of trees in the height of springtime,' declared Captain Hall of one calm, 'so numerous were the whistlers.' David Bone, as a young officer in the *Loch Ness* in the 1890s under the formidable 'Bully' Martin, remembered being caught in a calm in Cardigan Bay when Martin at once stamped upon the deck, pursing his lips in a coaxing 'Ssss – Sss – Shs-Shs!' On the square-rigger *Peking* in 1929 the German skipper, convinced all whistling was a bad-weather breeder, irritably yanked a fistful of hair from the head of a trilling deck-boy and banished him to the royal for two hours' penance.

'Russian Finns'

Calms brought into their full inheritance the 'Russian Finns', an embracive description for seamen from northern Europe, whose not least uncanny endowment was skill in controlling winds. About AD 900, Eric VI of Norway – 'Old Windy-Cap' – had governed the winds merely by turning about his cap; and his natural descendants were the 'Finns' (who perversely were often Germans or Swedes). Captain de Cloux, master of the *Herzogin Cecilie*, was one, suspected by brother captains of the ability to 'troller' or conjure weather at will. 'Can't fight trolldom,' said Sam Svenson of *Beatrice, Cecilie*'s racing rival. With Christianity's arrival, trolls, as the diminished nature spirits of the north, had secured immortality by conveying their magic to the 'Russian Finns'.

Distinguished among a Finn's tricks was to stick his knife into the ship's mast, towards the quarter from which wind was desired. Steel masts were sad hindrances to sorcery, but sailors were not unresourceful. In polished seas, Captain David Crowe of the *Semantha* was observed to whistle and to whittle a foot of deal as he walked the deck, a surrogate which he propped up abaft the mast before driving his knife-point into it.

Hesperus gossip recalled other charms. One becalmed skipper threw overboard every match in the ship bar one. This he lifted blazing to his cigar and the wind blew it out! An anticipatory halyard tapping against the mast or a he-goat's skin on a Hebridean fishing-boat (was not the storm-god Thor's chariot drawn by he-goats?) brought breezes. Icelanders obtained draughts by sacrificing on the mainsail lice picked from shirts. ('We may imagine that this remedy would not, in some ships, want for material for its application,' said a

Scottish skipper cattily.) To make clothes on board a ship assailed by foul winds merely 'sewed them on'; timely needlework tacked fair breezes in place.

For every sailing-ship proceeding about the high seas, a shark's tail nailed to the jib-boom, longer part uppermost, was an essential charm to the wind-gods. On her maiden voyage no sailing-ship wasted long in capturing such a tail. When the *Peking* lost hers (mysteriously, for it was firmly spiked fifty feet above the waves) there was general gloom: 'Our fair-weather charm and it's gone!'

As for cats, those accomplices in witchcraft, respected storm-raisers who carried 'gales in their tails', he who drowned one or dared to 'spit to windward or to call the cat a long-tailed bastard' was asking for trouble. As recently as 1949, on the 'last grain race', the *Passat*'s cat gave birth to five kittens. Two were kept 'to be brought up as good sea-cats'. As the unwanted kittens went overboard the wind suddenly veered dead against the ship.

For a Lapland witch a handful of sand tossed into the air concocted a malignant draught. 'Mair forecast in the concerns o' the great deep than a wise mariner ought to despise' was the verdict on the notorious witch Margery Forsythe of the Solway Firth; and Sir Walter Scott found Bessie Millie of Orkney so powerful that, 'he was a venturesome master of a vessel who left the roadstead of Stromness without paying his offering to propitiate Bessie Millie. Her fee was extremely moderate. Being exactly sixpence'.

The sale of winds, favourable for the mariner's own use, foul for rivals, was once a moneymaker. As late as 1861 Cornishman John Suttern provided winds, regretting only that 'trade had grown unprofitable' (steamers did not buy). In this department of magic, knots were common, derived perhaps from the silver string of Aeolus's wind-sack. Customers received thrice-knotted cords of which the first knot loosened gave a fair wind; the second, a storm; the third, a hurricane.

Lacking a witch, sailors 'bought' wind of the wind-gods, the sea itself, or its deities or saints. A traveller in 1822 saw a barrel of *sake* and a bag of copper coins sacrificed for the favour of Kompira, Japanese god of all the elements. As the USS *Columbus* crossed the Line the wind failed and while, on the quarterdeck, recalling Longfellow's lines the commodore intoned:

> Now all is ready, high and low,
> Blow, blow, good Saint Antonio!

below, the bosun sang: 'Blow, good devil, and you shall have the cook!' (Sea-cook's gifts were such that their sacrifice was easily contemplated.) Homeward bound in 1930 the crew of the four-masted barque *Olivebank* rashly washed clothes on Sunday, and every breeze went against them. Two packs of playing-cards were sacrificed overboard to change the wind, then, only fifteen miles from Ireland, came another breathless calm. In lieu of the cook himself, his best trousers were tossed overboard, 'a supreme sacrifice to fate . . . if this didn't work nothing would'. But it was unconvincing magic: the *Olivebank* was to spend two frustrating weeks, helplessly boxing up and down the Western Approaches.

Calming Storms

The belief that a storm would cease if a woman showed herself to it naked has already been mentioned. Less aesthetically Italians diminished a gale by exhibiting their bare backsides to it, and for friendly winds Frenchmen whipped the naked bottoms of cabin-boys at the mainmast on Monday mornings. Such rituals recalled human sacrifice to the sea, the last of which is ascribed to Vannes, Brittany, in the eighteenth century, when a child nailed up in a tub with a taper and holy water was delivered to the waves.

The sophisticated laughed, yet in emergencies were only too likely to join their simpler brethren in attempted placation. Caught in a Mediterranean tempest while on passage to Palermo in 1798 with Admiral Nelson, Count Esterhazy flung to the waters an expensive snuffbox bearing the likeness of his Italian mistress. Until the 1930s French fishermen used a rosary, string attached for easy retrieval. On Mediterranean coasts a glass of wine is still poured into troubled waters; Eskimos dilute a disturbed sea with a bucketful of fresh water; Scots fishermen 'kill' waves with a hand-wave. Baron Hubner in *A Ramble Round the World* (c 1880) wrote of a charm used in cyclone weather off Japan: 'The sky was iron-grey; to the west a curtain of the same colour but darker . . . in the air above the waves I suddenly saw a cloud of white flakes: they were little bits of Joss paper which the Chinese were throwing into the sea to appease their gods.' The word 'storm' is naturally never uttered; 'Don't name it if you don't want it! Give it a name and there's the ugly face of it.'

Sea-Gods and Saints

What of the gods to whom seamen's petitions were addressed? Leader of the pantheon was Poseidon or Neptune, lord of the seas, inventor of ships, whose underwater palace-cave in the deep Aegean glittered with gold, who gathered clouds and waves, calmed seas and granted safe passages. Represented as an old bearded man with a trident, trailing seaweed, he rode the foam in a divine chariot or car, drawn by frisking dolphins or by tritons, blowing conch-shells in his honour. These took their name from Triton, half-man, half-fish, son of Poseidon and his consort Amphitrite, female aspect of the sea, whose netted hair was dressed with crabs' claws.

From Oceanus proceeded all the watery element; his sister consort Tethys was greatest of the sea-goddesses; his 3,000 aquatic daughters the Oceanids. Proteus, guard to Poseidon's seal-herd, and Nereus, 'Old Man of the Sea', inferior only to Poseidon himself, were affably ready to assist sailors. Nereus's fifty daughters, the Nereids, were ancestresses of mermaids. In Scandinavian waters ruled the all-powerful Odin, who sent storms, and Njord, dweller in the shoreside 'place of ships', who held maritime pursuits in his hand. Almost a god and

Poseidon or Neptunus Rex, King of the Ocean, in his 'car' drawn by dolphins. He carries a trident, symbol of sovereignty and sea-power, which as such is also carried by Britannia

surrounded by booty from wrecks, sat the giant Aegir and his wife Ran, who stirred the waves to imperil vessels and cast a great net for every man who ventured upon the sea. To drown was 'to go to Ran'.

Wherever the sailor found himself, the gods were there: Viracocha, the 'white seafoam god' of Peru; O-Wata-Tsu-Mi, the Japanese 'Old Man of the Tide' whose messenger was a sea-monster; Tashire, Tawhiri-ma-tea and Taaruatai, Poseidons of the Society Islands; Tangaroa, with fish his children, the god of the Maoris. In the Hervey Islands, Vatea, half-man, half-shark, inventor of nets and fishing, and his brother Tirnivan, lord of fish, half-man, half-sprat, were esteemed. The Tahitians' prayer on setting sail was, *'Tahitia mai i te matou tere, e te atua!'* – 'Harken unto us throughout our voyage, O gods!' Varuna, a fish his sign, was the Indian Neptune. To the Chinese goddess, Ma Chua, whose shrine lamps provided protective ashes for junks, sailors called during storms as 'Grandmother Ma Chua!' The Arabs worshipped Kidir, brother of Elias, ruler of winds, god of voyages. The Hawaiian deities Kunra and Hina obligingly drove shoals of fish to the island in season. These were but a few among thousands.

The essence of all pagan ceremonies for sea-gods is contained in the voodoo ritual for Agwé Woyo, god of the sea, which survives in the West Indies. By the mast of a brightly flagged boat, oblivious to singing, drums, trumpets or conch, stands the *mambo*, holding up two white chickens in signal to Agwé. Two women fall possessed – the god has arrived! In rising din a ram is pushed overboard, the chicken are slaughtered and, with a seven-tiered wedding-cake, they join the offerings piled high in the model 'Agwé's barque'. With ritual consecration completed, six men heave the barque over the rail, it sinks like a stone, plucked down by the god's own hands, and everyone bursts forth in a great song of *réjouissance*.[56]

In many countries the coming of Christianity brought changes in honours; pagan petitions became the property of saints. Still, for the prudent mariner, old gods, if demoted and tamed to silence, lingered on. Odin, for example, was now transmuted as Old Nick, the sea-demon with a hundred aliases – Nokke, Neck and Nyck; and the Indian god Deva Lokka as Davy Jones, noted for his underwater 'locker'.

Among the newly powerful the Virgin Mary, 'a spiritual lighthouse', patroness of coastal chapels, became 'Our Lady Star of the Sea' and since the goddess Aphrodite ('risen from sea-foam') had been worshipped by the Greeks in seaside chapels, such an exchange was logical. St Anne was a gentler successor to Ahès, whose malevolence was only too apparent to the Widows of the Sea. Nevertheless recent observers of the *Tour de Paroisse* near St Malo and other Breton fishing ceremonies have been struck by their curiously joyless atmosphere of propitiation, never of light and joy; Christian admittedly, yet lacking in hope.

Among sailors' saints were the indispensable St Peter, St Bartholomew, St Ronald, St James the Great, patron of the Spaniards, and St George, petitioned by the Sardinians to repel the foes of the tunny-fish, St Michael, saint of wind, who won a diving contest with the Devil – and St Nicholas of Myra, who walked the water in seaweed boots. All were popular;

there was a saint for every need and season.

Some personages are strictly local. On Harrison Lake, British Columbia, the steamer *Lake Queen* passes Doctor's Point where in the rockwall stands the 'doctor', naturally white-coated and red-hatted, who, legend claims, was shot by a vengeful Indian in 1880 and turned to stone. Everyone 'feeds' the doctor by dropping crumbs into the lake. 'Let me tell you,' say the *Lake Queen*'s crew, 'once Jack took a fishing party on charter, and they scoffed at the legend and refused to follow the custom . . . On the way back a sudden storm came up and nearly swamped the lot of them. No sir, everybody on the lake knows enough to feed the doctor.'[57]

'Mackerel Skies and Mares' Tails . . .'

Even in an age of scientific forecasting a 'weather-eye' is respected; and, for small boats in particular, a feeling, superstitious or otherwise, for the sea's aspects, the wind and clouds, may still come abruptly and importantly into its own.

Of the thousands of weather axioms, highly local or worldwide, a handful must stand for all. As always the moon is a monitor; a broken incandescent halo of cirrus cloud around her presages storms which sailors believe come from the open side of the cloud ring. Backstays are part of standing rigging and 'sun's getting up his backstays' describes visible sunbeams linking sky to sea and promising ill-weather. Both common and reliable is:

> Rainbow to windward, foul fall the day
> Rainbow to leeward, damp runs away.

A sea-version of the doyen of weather jingles describes the 'sun-dog' or small rainbow on the horizon (especially if in the wind's eye):

> Dog in the morning, sailor's warning
> Dog in the night, sailor's delight.

And very dependable are the weather warnings:

> When the wind shifts against the sun
> Trust it not for back 'twill run
> When the wind follows the sun
> Fine weather will never be done,

and:

> Comes the rain before the wind
> Stays and topsails you must mind
> Comes the wind before the rain
> Your topsails you may set again.

From the direction in which the tails (or 'goats' hair') or cirrus clouds point, comes the wind:

> Mackerel skies and mares' tails
> Make lofty ships carry low sails.

In tropical waters, most perilous of all for sailing-ships, sailormen early learned to heed the glass:

> First rise after low
> Foretells a stronger blow.

A rise in barometric pressure merely announces the passing of a storm's centre; its full fury will recur, often after about half an hour, a useful interval for hurried repairs, more battening-down and a hasty meal, aptly called 'a dying man's dinner'. Another staple rhyme of the tropics, describes a storm's duration:

> Long foretold, long last
> Short notice, soon past.

Sea-residents are shrewd weather prophets:

> When the sea-hog jumps
> Stand by your pumps!

Leaping porpoises or 'sea-hogs' foretell storms – with water below decks. In the face of foul weather mullet swim south; sharks, seawards; cod swallow pebble ballast; cockles press it about them; sea-urchins thrust deep into mud. 'As soon as seafaring men observe them, they at once moor their ships with several anchors.' But the Portuguese man-of-war jellyfish signifies calms and the argonaut or 'paper nautilus' was pleasantly hailed by Pliny: 'O fish, justly dear to Navigators! Thy presence assures winds soft and kindly! Thou bringest the calm and thou art the sign of it!' It was the Greek sailor's fancy that about the winter solstice the kingfisher or 'halcyon' built her nest upon the sea which then remained calm until her eggs hatched. Thus 'halcyon days' of peace and happiness were unmarred 'by the wrinkle of the wave'.

> Seagull, seagull, stay on the sand,
> It's never good weather while you're on the land.

Seagulls inland or flying noisily spell coming storms – 'the higher the gulls, the harder the gale'. 'I like to see "old shellbacks" sitting low and not shrilling overhead with all sails set,' said a naval salvage officer in 1917, eyeing the sky and

Stormy petrel, a harbinger of rough weather, said, like St Peter, to be able to 'walk on water'

rightly foreseeing an interruption to his work. Tempests are nigh if the agreeably-named 'sailor's friend' that warns of storms is flying – the brown, white and black 'alamottie', 'storm-fish', 'Mother Carey's chicken', *'oiseau de Notre Dame'*, *'Aves Sanctae Mariae'* or stormy petrel (perhaps from Petrello 'little Peter', for like the saint petrels 'walk' on water).

St Elmo's Fire

'Some call it St Elmo's fire, others corposant. The balloons of light presage disaster. I'll be glad when another day comes up,' said George Grant's skipper in 1910, expressing the seaman's common sentiment about glowing flambeaux of static electricity on jackstaffs or crackling tongues of light racing up rigging. A fiery night like this made the toughest uneasy.

Under a plenitude of fifty names, with superstitious joy or terror, the display has been described since Graeco-Roman times, when its protective illumination was benevolently placed by Zeus about the heads of Castor and Pollux, Leda's Twins, the Dioscuri, during the stormy first voyage of the Argonauts. Its most common name, St Elmo's fire, perhaps derives from St Erasmus, saint of seamen, or from saints Ermyn, Telm or Anselmo. To some it was corposant, corruption of *corpo santo*, 'holy body' (in Scottish vernacular 'Corbie's aunt'). The French called it Hélène, the Germans Helenen Feuer, others Fermie's fire, Castor and Pollux, Leda's Twins, Firedrake, *Zeelicht*, *Wetterlicht*. Not everyone thought it holy. Grimly humourous Greek sailors called it *Telonia*, 'demon tax-gatherer', whose light destroyed rigging, masts and crews.

But generally it was agreed the light showed that St Elmo, protector of seamen, was near, warning of storms if moving downwards, or of improving weather if upwards. Columbus, da Gama, Magellan and Dampier all knew St Elmo's fire and cheered their crews with it; Magellan wrote of 'a great consolation to us during the tempest'. With 'Salve corpo santo!' Portuguese boatswains piped all hands to salute the fire and called five lights together 'Our Lady's crown'. Or the lights were the souls of dead shipmates; sailors avoided oaths while they burned.

Richard Henry Dana met it off Cuba, when in breathless air he and another clewed up the main topgallant sail and descended to find the whole crew staring upwards. At the masthead where they had stood was a ball of light. 'We were off the yard in good season, for it is held a fatal sign to have the pale light of the corposant thrown upon one's face'.

Waves and Waterspouts

Certain waves in the 'rote' had special qualities. The Celts believed that the powerful ninth reached shore before the rest; the Welsh that the dead were buried 'where the ninth wave breaks'. Water from the 'third die' was invaluable in woe-working. Pedigree hallows such beliefs: Allatius in *De Graecorum Hodie quandorum opinationibus* (1645), on passage from Messina to Malta, saw:

> ... the captain, who was accounted an experienced and skilful mariner, standing at the bow, while he muttered and pointed at something with his finger. I ... inquired what he was doing. The old man, with a cheerful countenance, answered, 'I am breaking the force of a fatal wave, and am making the sign of the cross, and saying the prayers proper for the occasion ... by so many waves by which the ship is tossed, none but the ninth can sink it'.

In Denmark and Ireland the 'moan of the sea' signified that the sea 'wanted one'; bluer than the surrounding water, *Naòldur* or 'death's breakers' portended Icelandic wreck. A crew lost by drowning caused a *Dauthalág*, a 'death's calm', on the waters; the sea was satisfied and other crews were safe.

Tides mirror life. A true sailor's heart beats faster with the flood tide and a sailor's child whose right hand is baptised with water from the flood tide will never drown. A growing tide produces those who will follow the sea-trade; boys favoured by birth at Christmas high tide become captains. If a fisherman's son is laid in a fish-basket immediately after birth with seashells beneath him and covered with a fisherman's jersey, he will reliably follow his father's footsteps. Even today in fishing communities a boy is half-expected if birth occurs at the rising tide, a girl with the ebb. As with life, so with death. Patients *in extremis* cannot die until the tide turns; death is easier with the ebb: *'s'en aller avec la marée'* say the Bretons.

Of waterspouts – *dragons de mer* – endangering small sailing-ships and ever feared by superstitious mariners, El Masudi reported, 'There are *timmins* or dragons in the Atlantic seas . . . black serpents, passing from the desert into the sea . . .' The version was popular. Oriental seamen, beating drums and gongs to frighten the spirits whose handiwork waterspouts were, enlarged imagination and declared that they had actually seen dragons ascending the watery column.

Until fifty years ago ingenious dispersals were commonly used. One square-rigger's master spoke of the sinister Atlantic 'Rains' on the Gulf Stream's edge, where lay light airs, violent squalls, lashing rain and waterspouts, and remembered that when one crossed his bow it snapped off the jib-boom and brought down the foretopgallant mast. Suddenly dozens of waterspouts circled the helpless ship. In time-honoured reply the brass four-pounder signal cannon was laid over the taffrail as the crew prepared – superstitiously – to 'shoot the dragon' and – practically – to 'jar the waterspout down'.

Medieval sailors, black-handled swords in hand and reading the Gospel of St John, knelt at the mainmast as the 'dragon' approached. At the words *'Et verbum carne factum est et habitant in nobis'*, they made the sign of the cross and, as though to cut the spout to ribbons, slashed the air. 'They say then, it is really cut, and lets all the water fall with a great noise,' wrote Thévenot in *Travels into the Levant* (1687). For the Greek sponge-fishers of Tarpon Springs, Florida, little changes. At the sight of a waterspout they carve a cross on the mast and thrust a seaman's knife into it to 'stab' the spout to death. A dreary penance awaits the desecrator of the Cross; but none hesitates to use the charm.

8 Sea-Words: the Sailor's Language

It is by way of a compliment to a spare and salty idiom that many sea-phrases – 'show a leg', 'cut of his jib', 'all hands on deck' – have drifted in to flavour land-speech. Conciseness is the hallmark of a sailor's language; a captain 'fights his ship' – deploys her to battle advantage; one ship 'speaks' another, today by radio, formerly – and perversely – by 'making her number', hoisting, colourfully rustling in the halyards, her *letter* flags of identification, and enquiring: 'What ship? How many days out? Where bound? Goodbye – and a pleasant voyage!' The ensign dipped; the ships proceeded; at home the wanderer would be reported 'all well'.

Greeks, Italians, Spaniards, French, Dutch, Scandinavians, Egyptians and other seafarers contributed to the windship's vocabulary. With romantic and expressive words the sailor could speak easily of his white-winged ship and her moods; of the savage Horn and of lambent Eastern nights; of his daily round and the joined shout at the halyards. The glance at the sailor's language which follows, can merely hint at its richness; William Falconer's *A New Universal Dictionary of the Marine* (1815) had 795 pages.

Round the Galley Fire

To the sailor, deprived of home comforts for months on end, little mattered more than ship's food. It was often execrable. Meat was tainted and tough, water addled in the cask. Admiral 'Jacky' Fisher recalled that in his young days the ship's biscuits were so full of life that midshipmen raced them across the gunroom table. 'Parish-rigged' vessels – frugal as parish relief ashore – put to sea ill-provisioned by 'nipcheese' owners. In a wry and much-adapted joke one crew read their owners' houseflag 'H & H' as 'Harsh and Hungry'.

Weather was an imponderable. Even in the most efficient of navies the worst could happen. Foul winds brought the crew of the USS *Iroquois*, very slow, 'rolling like a sinner in hell' and taking thirty-two days from Rio to the Cape, to their last ludicrous sea-stores – a peck of nutmegs! A horror story of 1881 told how Captain Kruger of the barque *Tiger* was repeatedly driven back by gales until, with all food gone, he killed his dog for the crew's dinner. He then offered to shoot himself for their next meal, but the chief mate delayed execution for a day, and in the nick of time, only 200 miles off the coast of Maryland, the British *Nebo* hove into view.[58]

Names revealed all. Before refrigeration maritime staples were salt-pork and salt-beef, 'salt-horse', 'salt-junk' or 'Irish-horse' – 'tougher than the bosun's hide' cried Captain Whitfield. 'With the kind of flavour you'd expect an Egyptian mummy to give off if it were boiled,' added AB Sam Noble who joined the Royal Navy in 1875. Sailors (perhaps never happy if deprived of a grouse) were convinced that any rubbish went into their salting tubs. Salt-beef was a remarkable substance: 'One of my messmates cut a half model of a frigate out of a piece, sandpapered, varnished, and then glued it to the ship's side above the bread barge. You couldn't have told it from mahogany,' said Noble. In hard times such models went into the pot.

In the British Navy salt-beef was withdrawn as a ration in 1904, but orders were given that supplies must be used up and with revolting tenacity they lasted until 1913. This was not a record: in HMS *Swallow* in 1877 'a cask of beef was actually discovered in our hold, whose mark and tally dated back to Trafalgar!'[59] Salt-pork lingered until 1926. Before boiling, the day's 'whack' was steeped in the 'harness-cask' of oak or teak with brass hoops, named for the meat's horsey associations. This was slower to remove itself from the scene. In HMS *Loch Tulla* in 1939, Comamnder D. A. Rayner found fresh meat unavailable at certain northern ports and remembered reading that ships so situated might demand a harness-cask. He applied to the paymaster-commander at Lyness. 'Good God, I don't suppose anyone has asked for a harness-cask since the last sailing-ship went out of commission.' But within a month, resurrected by an imperturbable commissariat from some sequestered store, the *Loch Tulla*'s cask duly appeared and meat was again prepared in the old style.[60]

Varying legends account for the British Navy's name of 'Fanny Adams' for the unloved ration of canned meat. In one a child, Fanny Adams, was murdered and dismembered at Alton in 1867 and later, when a sailor discovered a button in his dinner, the name 'Fanny Adams' became attached to the canned meat for ever more. Another unfortunate, 'Harriet Lane', suffering a similar fate (some said she fell into a vat at a canning factory) lent her name to merchant navy meals. Meat cans were nicknamed 'fannies', a name which was to stick to standard messtins.

In the same vein the Finns called tinned meat 'kabelgarn' or 'rope-yarn'. In the US Navy it passed as the familiar bouilli or 'bully-beef', with, as Captain A. T. Mahan, USN, recalled, the constant accompaniment of 'desecrated' potatoes. If possible salt-fish ('poor John', 'hairy Willie' or 'Block Island turkey') was even more disliked than salt-beef. Pleasanter and so named until the late nineteenth century was 'Albany beef', succulent sturgeon first drawn from the Hudson River by British tars during the American War of Independence.

However unappetising, every crumb was welcome. Sailors said superstitiously that to return food to the galley invited future hunger. Ingenuity made 'sea-pie' from salt-meat, fish and vegetables; 'twice-laid' from yesterday's salt-fish, potatoes and yams; 'midshipman's crab' from pickles, salt-beef, salt-pork, ground biscuit and cheese (his 'nuts' were broken biscuits). Standard dishes were baked 'cracker-hash' of crumbs, leftover pea-soup, and scraps; 'dandy-funk', a notorious hasty pudding of broken biscuits, weevils and molasses; 'lobscouse' of legend, a stew of salt-meat, raisins and biscuits, seasoned, said cognoscenti, with 'galley-pepper' – smuts which blew into the pots in rough weather. Familiar was 'acting rabbit pie' of beef and bacon ('acting' describing any dish faintly resembling a favourite on shore); sustaining and boring 'burgoo' or porridge; 'pea-do', pea-soup; 'figgy-duff' or raisin-pudding. (A wartime group on the deck of a small naval vessel in Loch Iver was dispiritedly examining the snow-covered peak of Ben Stack. The cook murmured: 'Just like one of my duffs.' 'And about as bloody hard,' said his friend.) 'One-eyed steak' or 'Spithead pheasant' was a kipper; the Dartmouth name for rissoles was 'beagle balls' – a libellous link with hounds culled from the college pack. Those still hungry after such dishes were advised to stick their heads over the rail for gasps of ozone: 'Them's wind puddings.'

Rare fresh bread was 'soft tack' or 'rooties'. 'Pantiles' or 'hard tack' the forty-two-holed ship's biscuits, notable for being occupied by black-headed weevils, resident in the ancient canvas bags in which pantiles were stored. ('Eat them, weevils and all,' said the experienced. 'They're fresh meat.') Hard and soft breads were not very different. One cook whose soft bread was 'harder than the hobs of hell' was forced to hide on the royal yardarm on bread-days, while apprentices pelted him with his own wares.

Such delicacies are no longer seen but irreverent nicknames for foods remain: 'Babies' heads' for a glutinous canned meat pudding; 'train smash' for canned tomatoes. In the US Navy about thirty years ago corned beef hash was 'Kennel ration' or 'Strongheart' (both famous dog-foods); 'billy-goat' described lamb and 'seagull' frozen chicken. Galley sensitivity was not excessive: 'niggers in a snowstorm' did for both curry and rice, and prunes and rice.

In hard times the traditional drink was 'Scotch coffee' – burnt bread boiled in water with sugar. Ambrosial for cold watchkeepers is the British Navy's 'ky' or cocoa made from slab cocoa. The first mug of coffee, 'Java', 'Jamoke' or 'Joe', drunk each morning was well-named 'coffee royal', and considered barely potable unless the condensed milk or 'tinned teat' (fresh milk being 'cow juice') was added so lavishly as 'to float a marlinspike'. This was seldom. One master recalled that on his first voyage he consumed at one sitting a tin of condensed milk. This he learned was his ration for three weeks!

Today's sail-training ships enjoy introducing their young crews to traditional ship's food. Such enthusiasm came late. Captain Whitfield swore ('through a nine-inch plank') that if he met some of the ships' chandlers of his day in his 'final anchorage' and they were not sizzling in the furthermost pit, feeding on 'Harriet Lane' and maggoty biscuits, he would forgo his grog ration for eternity!

Master-minding galley operations, and of unflattering reputation, was the ship's cook, often a pensioner, rarely with a full set of legs and eyes. (Arms were of course essential.) It was a sought-after job: 'All quartermasters, captains of tops etc, look forward to the cook, as cardinals do to the Pope.' He was known variously as 'Doctor', 'Drainings' or 'Slushy'. 'Son of a sea-cook' remains a telling insult. A US Navy tradition demands that in penance for a multitude of sins the cook carry on deck the seabags of any departing member of the crew. The cook's assistant was 'Jack Nastyface'.

Rumour related that members of this unadmired profession boiled to death the salt-meat to increase their perquisite of half the extracted 'slush' or grease. The rest went to the boatswain as ship's grease, or to the purser for 'pusser's dips' or candles. On American men-of-war barrelled slush was sold for the benefit of the ship '. . . usually going for beautifying'. The galley, one permitted spot for smoking, a 'mug-up' and gossip, gave its name to a 'buzz' or rumour, a 'galley-packet' or later a 'galley-wireless', born therein. Another natural gathering-place, the 'scuttlebutt', where the crew's fresh water ration was stored, also lent its name to rumour.

For centuries the lack of 'fresh-mess' in the sailor's diet caused scurvy. The mandatory issue of lime-juice which ended the disease gave rise to the name 'lime-juicer' for the British ship, and 'limeys' for her sailors. Allowances of food and water were 'pound and pint' or 'Board of Trade whack' since the Board stipulated the meagre quantities. Captain Whitfield recalled rations when he was a cadet in 1887: five Liverpool pantiles a day; $\frac{3}{4}$lb salt-meat a day (with twice a week 1lb Harriet Lane); $\frac{1}{4}$lb soft tack twice a week; 2lb sugar weekly; $\frac{1}{2}$lb canned butter or 1lb marmalade. In hard times these allowances were stretched to 'six upon four' or worse:

> Messing 'four among two' of us,
> Thank God there are but few of us!

when rations for two fed four. 'Living on bare navy' described those subsisting on standard rations, with no extras.

Dramatis Personae

The captain appears as the 'Old Man' or 'Owner'; the first lieutenant as 'Jimmy the One' or 'Number One'. The first mate of a merchant ship was always 'Mr Mate'. Many young naval officers benefited from the guidance of a 'sea-daddy' in early days at sea, just as Horatio Nelson had enjoyed the friendly support of Captain William Locker, RN.

Warrant or 'standing' officers carried the trenchant name 'salt-beef squires' and, unintentionally unflattering, 'idlers' was the word for non-watchkeepers such as coopers and blacksmiths. Head of the ship's police, the master-at-arms is 'Jaunty' (in the US Navy 'Jemmy Legs') derived, it is said, from the French *gendarme* and 'John Damme'. His assistants are 'crushers'. With perhaps the oldest of all nautical titles, the 'boatswain' or 'buffer' in charge of sails, rigging, anchor and cables was, because of his call, 'Tommy Pipes' or the 'Spithead Nightingale'. Gossip proclaimed boatswains as capable of a multitude of tricks, their unpopularity enhanced by unwelcome summonses to work, their disciplinary 'three sisters' and, through their mates, unpalatable connections with the 'cat'. With both will and opportunity for acquisition and disposal at benefit to themselves, they sold the ship's nails, paint and cordage, said sailors, in trade so brisk that a coloured 'rogue's yarn' was laid up in rope to obstruct peculation. One notable British boatswain, Johnny Bone, provided a verb, 'to bone', and an anecdote: 'He would stick at nothing. It is related that the late Lord Duncan, when he commanded the *Edgar*, once said to him: "Whatever you do, Mr Bone, I hope and trust you will not take the anchors . . ." '[61]

When ships were wooden and all water and many provisions (including the precious rum) travelled in casks, 'Chips' the carpenter and 'Jimmy Bungs' the cooper were indispensable. To radio operators clings the early twentieth-century nickname of 'Sparks', a reminder of radio's beginnings at sea. Modern are the US Navy's 'deck apes' for deck gang; 'snipes' for engine crews and 'pork chops' for supply officers. In coaling days the 'black gang', 'ash cats' or 'bunker cats' were stokers or firemen and the name may have passed to the engineering group. They were curiously linked with the padre, 'sky-pilot' or 'devil-dodger', because everyone on board barring only the captain, the sick and, in theory, the padre, helped in coaling. In fact the padre was always first to join in, donning ceremonial white gloves to wheel his first barrowload.

The gunner, in charge of the 'Bengal lights' which preceded modern signalling, was 'Old Blue Lights'; the navigating officer or 'Pilot' professionally concerned with 'flying the blue pigeon' or sounding lead (shirkers 'swung' rather than cast the lead), was 'Old Soundings'. Since he was also responsible for the water-tanks his assistant may still be 'Tankey'.

At the foot of the ship's social ladder were juniors, midshipmen, 'scabs' or 'warts' (more formally 'young gentlemen'). A senior requiring a messenger would shout jovially 'W.O.D.' for

'Wart of the Day'. They were also 'snotties', allegedly because they substituted sleeves for handkerchiefs. For their brass buttons, merchant navy apprentices were 'brassbounders'.

In navies legend blew richly about pursers or 'pussers', those officers responsible for pay, clothing and provisions. Like boatswains their prime occupation was said to be fiddling and profiting from helpless sailors (until the early nineteenth century Royal Navy pursers were in fact officially permitted to benefit from transactions – and apparently did so in both sanctioned and unsanctioned ways). Not until the 1840s were pussers to emerge as irreproachable paymasters. Suspicion crystallised in the nickname 'Mr Nipcheese'. Only pussers, said crews, 'could make a dead man chew' – draw rations for a deceased or 'run' sailor. The 'Sailor's Complaint or the True Character of the Purser of a Ship' of about 1710 expressed popular views:

> As his name foully stinks, so his butter rank doth smell,
> Both hateful to sailors, scarce good enough for hell:
> The nation allows men what's fitting to eat,
> But he, curse attend him, gives to us musty meat;
> And bisket that's mouldy, hard stinking Suffolk cheese,
> And pork cut in pounds, and pork cut in pounds for to eat with our pease.

The word 'pusser', brimming with derogatory disciplinary undertones, is still good for a laugh. A 'pusser's name' – a *nom de guerre* given to avoid arrest; 'like a pusser's shirt on a handspike' – an ill-fitting suit from the store – on man or mast; 'a pusser's medal' – a food stain on clothing; 'pusser's crabs' – uniform boots; 'pusser's tricks' – illimitable! ('Should have been brought up a missionary – could convert anything,' was the judgement on one.) They have many connections with foods, usually disliked. In the war one mess cook in a destroyer was told 'where to shove his pusser's peas' until a kindly shipmate pointed out that this was grossly unjust – the poor chap already had twelve 'Chinese wedding-cakes' to go there from the day before. In the merchant service the word purser, shorn of its sting, describes the officer supervising the ship's finances.

'Dusty Boy' or 'Breadroom Jack', the purser's erstwhile assistant, may still be encountered as 'Jack Dusty' or in the USN as 'Jack of the Dust', the stores rating. Incompetent seamen despairingly assigned to waiting upon shipmates were dismissed as 'Fo'c's'le Peggies' or 'cherrypickers'. The 'Lady of the Gunroom' was the midshipman's servant.

Provisioning agents ready with everything from maps to marmalade were described as 'ships' chandlers'; but today the term has generally been superseded by the duller 'ships' supplier'. The 'slop chest', so essential a part of sailing-ship life, must also be mentioned. From the chest set up 'before the mast' were sold (often by the captain, at profit to himself) clothes, seaboots, oilskins and necessaries such as soap and tobacco. Trade was particularly brisk with those who had joined the ship belatedly in what was called a 'pierhead jump', with few clothes except those they stood up in.

'Show a Leg – or a Pusser's Stocking . . .'

Fair winds or foul, calms or great gales, watchkeeping went ahead. 'Warming the bell' or 'flogging the glass' were watchkeepers' hopeful tricks. Rumour held that to warm the half-hourglass in the hand caused the sand to flow faster and brought hammocks nearer. On men-of-war the immortal words 'Watch ahoy! Show a leg – or a pusser's stocking! Rouse and shine. It's tomorrer morning and the sun's scorching your bloody eyeballs out!' began the day, dating from days when wives – acting or official – came on board in port and female legs or stockings thrust from hammocks dispensed the occupants from rising. The phrase long survived the banning of the practice. A male sleeper loath to move was threatened with 'Out or down there!' – his hammock might be cut down under him. 'Blowing the grampus', throwing a bucket of water over the sleeper, also galvanised the tardy.

At 'lash and stow!', hammocks were rolled up for the day and the area made clear for use. Only thus were large crews accommodated. In the merchant service, a sailor in the forecastle enjoyed the superior comfort of a bunk with a lumpy mattress of straw – a 'donkey's breakfast', or one stuffed with 'carpenter's feathers', wood shavings.

Naval hammocks, spread by 'clews', were strengthened when a man intimated his intention of taking a wife and a naval way of announcing a marriage is to say that 'B—— is fitting a double clews'. 'Getting spliced' carries the same cheerful message:

> That girl who fain would choose a mate,
> Should ne'er in fondness fail her,
> May thank her lucky stars if fate
> Should splice her to a sailor!

sang Charles Dibdin. Hammocks are rarely seen today but newcomers to a ship are still granted twenty-four hours free of duty to 'sling their hammocks'.

Crews found the spaces between guns handy for amorous encounters with women allowed on board and, in course of time, they were convenient for the resulting births. Thus the words 'son of a gun' still cast doubts on a man's ancestry. If the cook was amenable, the galley was another comfortable corner for assignations and a comprehensive definition of a man-o'-war's-man was: 'Begotten in the galley, born under a gun, every hair a ropeyard, every tooth a marlinspike, every finger a fish-hook, and his blood right good Stockholm tar!'

The complicated business of ship-working supplied many picturesque phrases. When working aloft, rarely safe, beginners were advised to give 'one hand for the ship and one for yourself', to hold on with one hand and to work with the other. In naval circles 'one hand for yourself, one for the king' was proper and, in crises, 'two hands for the king'. Still, many lived flamboyantly, scorning the 'lubber's hole' and going aloft over the futtock shrouds. The *trou de chat* was for those deficient in courage, who might expect a 'dose from the foretopman's bottle' (more recently just 'the bottle') or to be 'brought up with a round turn'. Topmen and yardmen, the *corps d'élite* of the lower deck, were recognised by the 'foretopman's crest', a patch on the trousers' seat, the most likely part of their anatomy to be seen by their shipmates.

'Make and mend' piped the crew to repairing and making clothes, using sewing materials stored with keepsakes and letters in small, wooden 'dittyboxes'. Later the term, like 'ropeyarn Sunday', came to denote a half-day's holiday, a standeasy. But a 'negro's holiday' meant nothing but a hard Sunday's labour as enjoyed by plantation workers. Those released for a 'run ashore' – a short freedom – are 'libertymen'; those confined to the ship and viewing a port's charms through a glass enjoy 'fourth-class liberty'. One unfortunate, after seeing his shipmates hold a 'tarpaulin muster' – pooling their finances for a shore outing by tossing money into a tarpaulin sheet – was left behind to maintain the solitary 'baboon watch'.

'Tiddly' remains a useful naval word, conveying extra smartness in such matters as a sailor's shore-going suit, or ropework. Visiting the ship, Queen Elizabeth the Queen Mother knowledgeably congratulated Leading Seaman Les Kegg, **HMS** *Bronington*'s 'buffer', on his 'tiddly' coiled ropes on the sweep deck. Royal Navy ships still boast experts in this tradition. From seventy fathoms of condemned headrope **HMS** *Hecate* recently made the 'largest doormat in the world', which 'tiddly' masterpiece, displayed at the head of the gangway during a visit to Gibraltar, raised £50 for charity.

Rope 'cheeses' are 'tiddly' (the opposite of ropey confusion, a 'snakes' honeymoon'); so was braided 'sennit' work, used for chafing gear, log lines, and sailors' hats. 'Paunch mat', 'puddening' or the famed 'baggy-wrinkle' of worked yarns also prevented chafing and, in foul weather, 'body and soul lashings' about ankles and wrists kept the sea out.

Ships that are friendly rivals, perhaps launched and worked up together, are 'chummy ships'. Friends sharing 'brightwork' chores and polishing rags are 'raggies'; if they quarrel they 'part brass rags'. A focus of their attention was 'Charley Noble', the brass or copper chimney to galley or wardroom stove, named, said legend, for a shadowy shipmaster with a fancy for gleaming metal. On USS *Columbus*, Charles Nordhoff saw 'Charley Noble's face scoured as bright as a new doll's every morning'. In the US Navy 'to shoot Charley Noble' was to clean the chimney of soot by firing a pistol up it.

Larger 'holystones' or deck-scourers were 'handbibles', smaller ones, 'prayerbooks'. The source of the name is mysterious; were broken tombstones once used (as some say)? or did the prayerful pose of scourers suggest the name? or was it Sunday work?

Six days shalt thou labour and do all that thou art able,
And on the seventh holystone the decks and clean the cable.

And equally irreverent:

Eight bells had struck. The watch came from below
To bend the knee and neck
Though not to prayer, but to curse and swear
And holystone the deck!

As ever the work-shy, scroungers or 'galley rangers' appeared 'in everybody's mess but in nobody's watch', although generally comradeship was a notable feature of sea-life, exemplified in such toasts as: 'A sailor afore a landsman and a shipmate above all!' and, more fully: 'Messmate before shipmate, shipmate before soldier, soldier before dog!' In friendly insult sailors call soldiers 'pongoes' – a favourite rebuke was 'Sodgerin' young idlers!' In turn soldiers called sailors 'baggies', 'blues', 'dabtoes', 'flatfoots' or 'webfoots'. The general contempt of the sailor for those unfortunate enough to be landsmen is well expressed in the old rhyme:

One night came on a hurricane, the sea was mountains rolling,
When Barney Buntline turned his quid and said to Billy Bowling,

'A strong sou'wester's blowing, Billy, can't you hear it roar now?
Lord help 'em, how I pities all unhappy folks on shore now.'

Seamen worked 'roundly' or 'cheerly' – heartily, and 'handsomely' – carefully, hoping for the chance of a snooze or 'caulk' as the day went by. Deck seams, running fore and aft, were 'caulked' with rope-yarn and sealed with hot pitch. Thus, fore and aft, did the sailor also hope to arrange himself. 'The devil to pay and no pitch hot' and 'between the devil and the deep sea' are caulkers' sayings: 'devils' are the notoriously awkward upper outboard strake and garboard seams; 'to pay' came from the French *peier* 'to pitch'. 'At loggerheads' described a state of conflict – iron loggerheads, used to melt pitch, made lethal weapons.

Nautical parlance is rich in national prejudices. A loose rope-end, a frayed ensign or pendant, or sailors' clothing trailing from a bunk, are 'Irishman's or Dutchman's pendants'; a 'Frenchman' (of corkscrew reputation?) the occasional left-handed loop necessary when coiling down wire right-handed. Dutch sailors were invested with 'Dutch courage' through the medium of 'square-faced' gin before action. To make fast a rope or to belay rope insecurely is 'to hang Judas'.

'Waisters', 'sea-labourers', 'monkey's orphans' or 'longshoremen' described those fit only for coolie work in the ship's waist. Name-calling reflects curiously on the ancient link between sailors and farmers, both practitioners of trades concerned with harvests and hostile elements. 'Haymaking son of a sea-cook – bloody farmer!' sprang readily to the mate's lips, joining contempt with envy for the landsman's soft lot. 'Who wouldn't sell a farm and go to sea,' is the seaman's morning litany. When an escorting destroyer accidentally touched another ship in dirty Atlantic weather and the victim signalled curtly, 'What are you going to do now?' the instant response was, 'Buy a farm!'

'As handy as a cow in a spitkid!' was the nautical equivalent of a bull in a china-shop. Spitkids were the wooden tubs that did duty as spittoons in the days of chewing tobacco. The work-shy followed 'Tom Coxe's traverse' – 'up one hatch and down the other', hiding in the 'heads' and other corners to avoid work. An eighteenth-century ballad had a word of advice:

> 'All hands, unmoor,' the boatswain calls,
> And he pipes at every hatchway,
> If you Tox Coxswain's traverse tip him,
> Take care he don't catch ye.

Coxe (or Coxswain) was unidentified: some believed him the same novice who took three weeks to beat round the South Foreland. Tom Collins was another mystery, a nautical Hobson: 'to do a thing for Tom Collins' meant there was little choice. Awkward and argumentative is a 'proper Jack Adams', and 'Tom Pepper', say those who know, was kicked out of Hell, for being a bigger liar than Satan.

Crimps and Bucko Mates

If British ships were 'lime-juicers' Americans were 'Yankee hellships', 'blood packets' or 'slaughterhouses'. A crew's nationalities scarcely touched their allegiances – a typical sailing-ship might carry British, Bluenosers from Nova Scotia, Americans, 'Russian Finns' (Baltic seamen were also 'Yaw-yaws'), Portuguese, Germans and Dutch (often considered jointly: 'Fritz and Dutchy' was a common nickname; collectively they were sometimes known as 'Yah-for-Yes-folk'). An inevitable Swede and a negro cook completed the crew. All negroes were 'niggers'; all Portuguese, Spanish and South Americans were 'dagoes'. Such motley shipmates were usually securely bound under the Stars and Stripes or Red Ensign and ready to patronise those less favoured.

Contempt was often reciprocal. Americans scorned British ships; Bluenosers could not abide Americans, the British or Australians, let alone the Spanish or French. To the British other races, especially 'Dutchmen', were 'unreliable in tight corners'. All, except the British, professed contempt for the British Merchant Shipping Acts whose wise provisions required that crews sign on before a government 'shipping master', disposing of the notable scourge of 'crimping'.

When seamen were hard to come by, 'crimps' or boarding-house keepers, working to an ignoble pattern, undertook to provide crews. About 1890 when the *Loch Ness* anchored at San Francisco, the crimps' boats soon clustered under her bow while in the forecastle runners plied the men with booze and grand tales of jobs. Boats pulled ashore laden with drunken seamen, a year's pay at their belts and eager for a good time. Theft of wages, doping, 'shanghai-ing' ('Shanghai' Brown was a notorious crimp) might follow. Victims (for whom captains paid out 'bloody money' deducted from the man's wages so that it might be months before he earned a penny), were manhandled on board those ships which had requisitioned them. The coerced came to their senses at sea, to face months of the mate's fist and boot. The old chanty described the miseries thus:

> As soon as the clipper had got out to sea,
> Away-hay-blow the man down;
> I'd cruel hard treatment of every degree,
> Give us a chance to blow the man down.

Men had jumped overboard to escape such bullying. Those from 'Yankee packets' were instantly recognisable, said legend. One, typically, wore an ugly scar from temple across an empty eye-socket to mouth – the relic of a mate's knuckleduster. To have survived service in a 'hellship' conferred distinction. Skippers who attempted to dispense with crimps' services might find themselves beaten up or their vessels damaged, and most, of necessity, tolerated the system. Life at sea under any flag was no bed of roses but crimping added immeasurably to the miseries. Still, not every crew was cowed; enterprising apprentices from the *Springburn* once disposed of 'Shanghai Brown' himself by knocking him out and shipping him away on a China clipper!

'Bucko' was the epithet for Yankee mates, disciplinary experts at 'working-up' and 'manhandling' crews, who 'ate a sailor every morning and picked their teeth with the frayed end of a wire hawser.' On one immaculate snowy-decked ship the mate actually bit off the ears of erring sailors. The exhausted fell to their deaths from icy Cape Horn yards; or lost finger-nails battling with sails to 'Get 'em up! What she can't carry she may drag'. Ships, as sorely-driven as men, often lasted no longer than five years. Some Yankee captains, 'hard-cases', were nicknamed 'Bully'. Punishment came the way of few, not even 'Bully' Waterman, a 'human gorilla' with a 'persuader' at his wrist who, Fokke-like, padlocked his topsail sheets. A word must go to James H. Williams (1864–1927), an American negro seaman, who painted the blackest of pictures:

> What a pity that such an inspiring marvel of elegant perfection, delicate grace, usefulness, and majestic power should be made a floating torture-house, a 'blood packet', a beautifully sculptured shelter for human misery, grief, and despair, inhuman, fiendish cruelty, and wanton, unrestricted barbarities.[62]

One captain, 'land-saint and sea-devil', shouted for a bucket of seawater as his ship cleared land: 'I'm washing off my shore face. Here's my sea face.' Tossing aside frock-coat and top hat he emerged, choleric, a brute. Again crews were not resourceless; the men of the hard-caser *Frederick K. Billings*, unable to contemplate a return round the Horn, dropped a paraffin lamp into their ship's hold at Iquique. Within sixteen minutes, scorching all near her, the *Billings* burned to the waterline and sank. The crew were saved, but lost every possession, willingly accepting this as a modest price to be shot of the mate.

Not every 'Bully' was American. 'Bully' Martin, a driver in the Loch Line's wool-clippers out of Glasgow, achieved, perversely, near hero-status in the halyard chanty:

> Ses I who's th'skipper o' that little witch?
> Way, hey-ee, blow th' man down!
> Ses he, Bully Martin, th'son of a bitch!
> Give us th'time and we'll blow th'man down!

There were endless arguments as to which ships were worst. Some gave the accolade to Bluenosers. 'Hunger and ease in British ships' said the experienced. Verdicts were close-drawn. 'Goddam nigger-drivin' Yank, miserable hungry lime-juicer' was one. An American on the *Bellands* declared that food at least was plentiful on his country's ships, but a Peruvian scolded, 'And a belaying pin for an appetiser. Limeys ain't the worst.' Wry jokes told of mates dishing up 'belaying pin soup' and 'handspike hash'. Belaying pins were used in securing running rigging.

But, reassuringly, sea-comradeship often managed to conquer prejudice. Captain Whitfield admired American generosity to the *Latimer*'s starving crew when lamp oil had tainted their provisions. An Italian brig had sold them a barrel of sour meal – at a cruel price. Then two days later they met the *Carrie Winslow*, which signalled 'Send a boat!' and provided everything needful – fresh vegetables (an unheard-of luxury) and, the final touch, a case of beer for the captain, with the American skipper's compliments. The American would not take a penny in payment.

Punishments

Brief mention must be made of stark and sinister nautical punishments, many of great severity. 'Bilboes' or 'irons' (once made from Bilboan steel, the best), found aboard sailing-ships until the later nineteenth century, confined prisoners' legs and long figured in the classic injunction 'Clap him in irons!' To be flogged over a gun – 'to marry the gunner's daughter' – was, with luck, 'goose without gravy', blood not being drawn, The 'cat o' nine tails' – *martinet* to the French, after the disciplinarian Marquis de Martinet – of thrice-knotted cords with a heavy rope handle, assaulted the bare backs of delinquents in almost every sailing navy. It was kept in a red baize bag (to disguise bloodstains), hence the minatory 'letting the cat out of the bag'. In crowded ships there was 'no room to swing a cat'.

The laggard up or down rigging was 'started' with a frayed rope-end or 'colt'. Three canes bound together made the 'three sisters', not banned until 1809. In 'flogging round the fleet', which might follow a court martial, the prisoner, lashed to a grating, was rowed to each ship in harbour in turn to receive twelve strokes of the cat from the boatswain's mate. The 'rogue's march' on the drums added to the horror for crews who had obeyed the call 'all hands to witness punishment'. Even more brutal was 'keel-hauling', said to have been introduced by the Dutch in the fifteenth century, when the victim was drawn on a line under a ship and up the other side. Many drowned during the ordeal. 'Ducking at the yardarm' was similarly sinister.

Sails and Seas

Square-riggers, under plain sail, set five (or six) sails on each mast; in ascending order these were course, topsails (upper and lower), topgallant, royal, skysail. Romantically expressive of the sailor's pleasure in favourable weather were the names of the sails then used, often called embracively 'cloud-cleaners' or 'kites'. There were 'studding-sails', 'angels' whispers' or 'angels' footstools'; 'trust-to-gods' or 'hope-in-heavens'; 'puffballs', 'savealls'; 'moonsails'; 'moonrakers', 'raffees' or 'skyscrapers' and 'fly-by-nights'. Along the bowsprit lay the enigmatically named 'Jamie Green'. Reaching almost to the sea were watersails and as fillings between sails were 'bonnets' and 'stockings' – 'Hoist a stocking to your jib and a bonnet to your topsail' to get the last 'onion', part-knot or 'Chinaman'. An apocryphal story is told of a smart Yankee clipper in which the Chinese cabin-boy threw a bucket of slops overboard windward of the mate, who angrily tossed him over as drogue to the log – describing the speed as 'ten and a Chinaman'.

When a ship was 'cracking on the dimity' tearing home from China with the 'first chop', the first of the new season's tea, defying typhoons and every act of God and man, the racing really began. The log of the *James Baines* once recorded: 'Ship going 21 knots with main skysail set,' still thought to have been the greatest speed ever attained by a sailing-ship. Then was every sail pressed into service. One triumphant crew, flying 'everything but the captain's night-shirt' as they tore up Channel in close company with a rival, rushed on deck with their blankets which they rigged to trap the last inch of wind.

Named, said some, for their value to trade (others claim the word derives from an ancient word for 'track') were the reliable 'trade winds', kingpins of the sailing world. In their domain, from about 30° North to 30° South of the Equator, were found white-capped, china blue seas, flying-fish slattering on board in flickering silvery showers for the crew's frying pan, under a light-filled azure sky. Ships enjoyed perhaps 1,500 miles of sun-kissed ocean passage in King Neptune's own realm, 'snoring along' in fair weather sails, day after day, 'low and aloft', 'every stitch she could carry', while sailors enjoyed 'flying-fish weather' and 'Jack's holiday', benison of the China trade.

In the great southern ocean the 'anti-trades' spin round the world from the west without interruption, making fearsome the east-west passage in Cape Horn seas. But shipmasters in the Australian trade liked the speed they gave on the long, lonely 'running the easting down' after the Cape of Good Hope. Then a ship under storm canvas, driving along at great speeds in thunderous, white-lashed following seas, 'taking it green', charged ever eastward in the latitudes called the 'roaring forties' with under the bow 'a bone in her teeth'.

About the Equator lie the heartbreaking 'doldrums', once with much 'pulley-hauley' for crews. The fastest passage could founder there while the creaking ship, reflected in bottle-end green waters, lay idle for days or 'ghosted', tar bubbling in her seams, and her crew, trimming sails and swinging yards, alert to catch the least catspaw in 'Paddy's hurricane' or an 'Irishman's gale', a dead calm. Then, suddenly, a vicious squall ripped sails to pieces. In the doldrums many a stout ship became a veritable wreck.

'Swallowing the Anchor'

At the end of his sea-career, the sailor 'swallows the anchor' and comes ashore, eventually to 'cut his painter', 'slip his cable' or 'go aloft'. He has 'unrove his lifeline'. If sea-burial should come without warning, through accident, or violence of sea or enemy, the sailor is 'gone to Davy Jones' whose roomy sea-bottom 'locker' swallows all ships, persons and articles lost at sea. This synonym for sea-death cannot be accounted for: 'Duffy' and 'Davy' are negro words for ghost; some say a pirate named David Jones pushed victims overboard; still more that the locker is named for Deva Lokka, the Hindu goddess of death.

The favoured shellback, so long at sea that barnacles grow on his back, looks forward not to a conventional heaven but to 'Fiddler's Green'. Thence go all with fifty years' sea-service, and the favoured with lesser time. To get there the sailor becomes a gull, flies to the South Pole and into an open hatch spinning with the earth's revolutions. Here he enters, finds 'Fiddler's Green' within, and settles down to a sailors' paradise where 'the drinks and the smokes are logged but never paid, there are pubs on every corner and steaks and plum duff every day' and where 'are gathered all the good-looking women of the world to fill the pots and pipes of sailormen'.

Thus, in his final and traditional fantasies the sailor crystallises some of the eternal pathos and loneliness, the wry humour, the imaginative naïvety, the delight in simple pleasures, which, as much as high drama, have marked the seafaring life of all fleets and all ages and which helped to form its distinctive folklore.

References

1 Samuel Drake, *Nooks and Corners of the New England Coast* (New York 1875), 240
2 Jean Lipman, *American Folk Art in Wood, Metal and Stone* (New York 1948), 25–49
3 Alec Rose, *My Lively Lady* (1968), 15
4 W. S. Chalmers, *Max Horton and the Western Approaches* (1954), 51
5 Lionel Casson, *Ships and Seamanship in the Ancient World* (Princeton 1971), 212, 344–60
6 William R. Anderson and Blair Clay, *Nautilus 90 North* (New York 1959), 206
7 *Atlantic Monthly*, November 1938
8 J. G. Lockhart, *Curses, Lucks and Talismans* (1938), 176–9
9 Alan Villiers, *Set of the Sails* (New York 1949), 228, 235
10 C. W. Domville-Fife, *Epics of the Square-Rigged Ships* (1958), 204
11 Denys Forrest, *Tea for the British* (1973), 137
12 Katharine Crosby, *Blue-water Men and Other Cape Codders* (New York 1946), 122
13 Holger Thesleff, *Farewell Windjammer* (1951), 231
14 Richard Hough, *The Pursuit of Admiral von Spee* (1969), 170
15 Archibald MacMehan, *Tales of the Sea* (Toronto 1947), 31–8
16 Commander C. H. Lightoller, *Titanic and Other Ships* (1935), 64–7
17 *Chronicle-Herald*, 21 September 1976
18 W. L. Speight, *Swept by Wind and Wave* (Cape Town), 169–71
19 A. S. Rappoport, *Superstitions of Sailors* (1928), 232–3
20 Gordon Campbell, *My Mystery Ships* (1928), 269–70
21 Ernest Gann, *Song of the Sirens* (New York 1968), 62
22 W. Ellis, 'Lonely Cape Hatteras, Besieged by the Sea', *National Geographic*, September 1969, 393
23 Michael Lewis, *Spithead* (1972), 199
24 Barry, James P., *Ships of the Great Lakes: 300 Years of Navigation* (Berkeley, California, 1973), 239

REFERENCES

25 Alton H. Blackington, *More Yankee Yarns* (New York 1956), 132–4
26 *The Times*, 24 December 1964, letter from Francis Newbolt; E. M. R. Ditmas, *The Legend of Drake's Drum* (Guernsey 1973)
27 Jerry Allen, *Sea Years of Joseph Conrad* (New York 1965), 244, 248, 322
28 Ms Allison Buchan and Mr I. C. MacGibbon, Wellington, New Zealand, personal letters, 16 February 1977 and 31 March 1977
29 A. D. Divine, *Dunkirk* (1945), 176–7
30 H. C. Adamson, *Keepers of the Lights* (New York 1955), 323
31 Hough, *The Pursuit of Admiral von Spee*, 127
32 I. Johnson, *Round the Horn in a Square-Rigger* (Springfield, Massachusetts 1932), 51
33 Florence Marryat, *Life and Letters of Captain Marryat* (1872), I, 37–8
34 E. W. Bush, *The Flowers of the Sea* (London 1962), 160; Forest J. Sterling, *Wake of the Wahoo* (Philadelphia 1960), 115
35 Crosby, *Blue-water Men and Other Cape Codders*, 158
36 Roger Keyes, *The Naval Memoirs: Scapa Flow to Dover Straits* (1935), 329
37 L. P. Lovette, *Naval Customs, Traditions and Usage* (Annapolis 1939), 253
38 Domville-Fife, *Epics of the Square-Rigged Ships*, 240–1
39 *Navy Times*, 28 February 1977 (By kind permission of the Editor)
40 A. T. Mahan, *From Sail to Steam: Recollections of Naval Life* (New York 1907), 51–2
41 Charles Nordhoff, *In Yankee Windjammers* (New York 1940), 108
42 A. B. Campbell, *Bring Yourself to Anchor* (1941), 212
43 Anderson and Clay, *Nautilus 90 North*, 225
44 T. Pasley, *Private Sea Journals, 1778–1782* (1931), 74
45 William R. W. Blakeney, *On the Coasts of Cathay and Cipango Forty Years Ago* (1902), 10
46 Robert Hastings Harris, *From Naval Cadet to Admiral* (1913), 20–22
47 Sterling, *Wake of the Wahoo*, 92–3
48 Lieutenant-Colonel Paul Neville, MVO, FRAM, RM, personal letter, 23 November 1976
49 Lightoller, *Titanic and Other Ships*, 112

50 Mahan, *From Sail to Steam*, 166
51 R. H. Bacon, *The Life of Lord Fisher of Kilvestone, Admiral of the Fleet* (New York 1929), 72
52 *American Journal of Science* 1820, I: 2, 178–9
53 Frank West, *Lifeboat Number Seven* (1960), 164
54 Anderson and Clay, *Nautilus 90 North*, 121
55 John Herries McCulloch, *A Million Miles in Sail* (New York 1933), 110
56 Harold Courlander, *A Treasury of Afro-American Folklore* (New York 1976), 32–5
57 Kay Alsop, 'The Queen Comes Calling', *Province*, 9 October 1976
58 Allen, *Sea Years of Joseph Conrad*, 120
59 Henry Baynham, *Before the Mast* (1971), 204
60 D. A. Rayner, *Escort* (1955), 47
61 Michael Lewis, *A Social History of the Navy 1793–1815* (1960), 265
62 James H. Williams, *Blow the Man Down!* (New York 1959), 46

Bibliography

Adamson, Hans Christian. *Keepers of the Lights*, New York 1955

Anson, Peter F. *Fishing Boats and Fisher Folk on the East Coast of Scotland*, London 1930; *Mariners of Brittany*, 1931

Armstrong, Warren. *Sea Phantoms*, 1956

Bassett, F. S. *Legends and Superstitions of Sailors and the Sea*, Chicago 1885

Beckett, Captain W. N. T., DSC, RN. *A Few Naval Customs, Expressions, Traditions and Superstitions*, Portsmouth n.d.

Benwell, Gwen, and Waugh, Arthur. *Sea Enchantress: the Tale of the Mermaid and Her Kin*, 1961

Bisset, James. *Sail Ho*, New York 1958; *Tramps and Ladies: My Early Years in Steamers*, New York 1959; *Commodore, War, Peace and Big Ships*, New York 1962

Bone, David. *Landfall at Sunset*, 1955; *The Brassbounder*, 1910

Bowen, Frank C. *Sea Slang*, 1929

Bradford, G. *The Mariner's Dictionary*, New York 1972

Broome, Captain Jack, DSC, RN. *Make a Signal*, 1955

Bush, Captain Eric Wheeler, DSO, DSC, RN (Retd). *The Flowers of the Sea*, 1962

Campbell, Commander A. B., RD, RN. *Customs and Traditions of the Royal Navy*, Aldershot 1956; *Bring Yourself to Anchor*, 1941

Casson, Lionel. *Ships and Seamanship in the Ancient World*, Princeton 1971; *The Ancient Mariners*, New York 1959

Dana, Richard Henry Jr. *Two Years Before the Mast*, New York 1946

Gould, Lieutenant-Commander R. T., RN (Retd). *The Case for the Sea-Serpent*, 1930

Hagelund, Albert Van. *La Mer Magique*, Verviers 1973

Kemp, Peter (ed). *The Oxford Companion to Ships and the Sea*, Oxford 1976

Knight, Frank. *The Clipper Ship*, 1973

Lovette, Lieutenant-Commander L. P., USN. *Naval Customs, Traditions and Usage*, Annapolis 1939.

Mahan, Captain A. T., USN (Retd). *From Sail to Steam: Recollections of Naval Life*, New York 1907

Nordhoff, Charles. *In Yankee Windjammers*, New York 1940
Rappoport, Angelo S. *Superstitions of Sailors*, 1928
Robinson, Commander Charles Napier, RN. *The British Tar in Fact and Fiction*, 1909
Rogers, Stanley. *Sea-lore*, c 1928
Sebillot, Paul. *Légendes, Croyances et Superstitions de la Mer*, Paris 1886–7; *Le Folk-lore des Pêcheurs*, 1901; *Contes de Marins*, 1882
Slocum, Captain Joshua. *Sailing Alone Round the World*, New York 1972
Smyth, Vice-Admiral W. H. *Sailor's Word Book*, 1867
Speight, W. L. *Swept by Wind and Wave*, Cape Town n.d.
Walker, Lieutenant-Commander C. F., RN (Retd). *Young Gentlemen: the Story of Midshipmen . . .* , 1938
Wells, Rear-Admiral Gerard, RN. *Naval Customs and Traditions*, 1934
Whitfield, Captain G. J. *Fifty Thrilling Years at Sea*, 1934
Whymper, F. *The Sea: Its Stirring Story of Adventure, Peril and Heroism*, 4 vols, n.d.

PERIODICALS
American Neptune
Mariner's Mirror
Nautical Magazine
Navy News
Navy Times
Sea Breezes

Index

Page numbers in *italics* denote illustrations

Acteon, 113
Ajax, 103
albatross, 149-50
Alert, 45
Amsterdam, 15
amulets, 76-88
anchor, 82
Anderson, Cdr William K., 146
Annie E., 66-7
Ariel, 46
Arlington, 48-50

Bacchante, 59-60
Barracouta, 54
Bayshimo, 55
Billings, F.K., 180
Biloxi Shrimp Festival, *98*
Bissett, Capt James, 77
Blakeney, Capt W.R.W., 113
blessing boats, 30-4, 98-9, *98*
Bluenose II, 14, 33, 34, *34, 35*
boatswain's call, 120-1
Bone, Comm Sir David, 24, 130, 152-3
Brandywine, 27
Britannia, 51, 105
Broadsword, 33
broom, 91
Bronington, 103, 124, 175
Brownson, Admiral W.H., 121
Brunswick, 19
bucko mates, 178-81
burial at sea, 108-110
Bush, Capt E.W., 122

Cadmus, 23
Calpean Star, 149-50
Campbell, Cdr A.B., 149
Campbell, Vice-Admiral Gordon, 60-1
Camperdown, 67-9
Cape Hatteras, 65
Cape Horners, 122-3
Carrie Winslow, 181
cats, 84-7, 92-3, 154, *85*
caul, 77-8
Charles Haskell, 71
christening; babies, 108; ships, 23-34
Christmas, 102-3
Churchill, 77, 134

Clan McLeod, 22
coins; in keel, 15; in mast-step, 10, 34-6, *35*
Columbus, 155, 176
Colossus, 36-8, *37,* 110
commissioning, 104
Conrad, Capt Joseph, 73-4
Constellation, 101
Constitution, 20, 27, 32, 76, 105
Conway, 100
cook, 169
Coorong, 50
corposant, 162-3
Countess, 29
Countess of Dufferin, 48-50
Cradock, Rear-Admiral Sir Christopher, 77
crimps, 178-81
'crossing the Line', 111-18, *111*
Cutty Sark, 16, 22, 38

Daedalus, 130-2
Dana, Richard Henry, 109, 123, 163
Davy Jones' locker, 184
days, taboo, 14, 29, 76, 88-90
'dead horse', 101-2
death at sea, 108-10
decommissioning, 104
Dixon, Capt G.C., 149
dolphins, 144-6
Dönitz, Admiral Karl, 61
Downs, the, *62*
Drake, Sir Francis, 70-1, 152
drowning, 36, 69, 77-8, 82, 110
Dunraven, 60

Empress of Ireland, 42
Eurydice, 21
eye of Horus, *16,* 17-18

farewell ceremonies, 121-4
Fiddler's Green, 184
figureheads, 18-23, *21*
Filby, 'Phil', COEMN, 83-4, *83*
fire-ships, 55-7
first fruits, 99
fish, 78, 147-8, *139, 146, 147*
Fisher, Capt 'Jackie', 124, 166

INDEX

fishermen's beliefs, 17, 96-9, 147-8, *16*
flags, 118-121, 165
Flying Dutchman, 54, 58-61
food, 166-70
footings, 100-1

galley, 166-70
Garthpool, 102
George's Bank, 70, 72-4, 130
ghost-sailors, 67-75
ghost-ships, 53-75
Gift Horse, 45
Good Friday, 109
Good Hope, 77
Goodwin Sands, 61-4
Grace Harwar, 43
Grand Duchess, 19
'Great American Sea-Serpent', 18, 128-30
Great Britain, 48
Great Eastern, 38-9, *49*
grog, 105-6
Guinness, Arthur, Son & Company, fleet, 32

Hall, Capt Basil, 109, 144, 152
Halsey, Capt Lionel, 78-80
Hartford, 32
Hecate, 85, 86-7, 175
Herzogin Cecilie, 47, 153
homeward bound, 121-24
Hood, 111, 114-18

Île de France, 51
Illawarra, 44
Imperator, 23
Implacable, 51
Intrepid, 112
Invincible, 32
Isadore, 23, 56

James Baines, 183
Jonahs, 92-3
Joseph Somers, 59

keel-laying, 13-14
Kelly, 52
Kidd, Capt., 64-5
Kipling, Rudyard, 75, 145
krakens, 126-7, *127*

Lady Grania, The, 32
Lady Gwendolen, The, 32
Lady Luvibund, 63-4
Lady Patricia, The, 32
Lake Queen, 159
language, 165-85
Latimer, 181
launching, 29-34, *31*
Leviathan, 39

lighthouses, 74-5
Lightoller, Cdr C.H., 50, 136, 141
Lively Lady, 25-6
Loch Ness, 152, 179
Loch Tulla, 167
Luce, Capt John, 71

M'Quhae, Capt Peter, 129-33, *131*
Mahan, Capt A.T., 54, 106, 123, 136, 167
maiden voyage, 40-3
Malaya, 36
Marryat, Capt Frederick, 89
Mary Celeste, 90
mascots, animal, 84-8, *85, 86*
mascots, other, 76-84
Masefield, John, 100
Mauretania, 46, 51-2
Maynard, Capt H.W., 87
mermaid, 15, 138-43
Miranda Guinness, 32
Mormacsun, 17
Morning Cloud, 39-40, 44
Morton, Lieut-Cdr 'Mush', 91
mourning, 12, 108-110

N.B. Palmer, 19
nautical phrases, 165-84
Nautilus, 29, 112
naval customs, 100-24
Nelson, Admiral Lord, 71, 155, 170
Neptune (Poseidon), 26, 30, 88, 110-18, *111,* 156, *157*
Neville, Lieut-Col Paul, 122
New Year, 103-4
New Zealand, 78-80
nicknames, 27
Northampton, 124
Northumberland, 62-3

oculi, *16,* 17, 78, *137*
Odysseus, *137,* 138, 149, 151
Olivebank, 89, 144, 155
Oliver Hazard Perry, 26
Omba, 93
Oriskany, 104
Osiris, 76
Otago, 73-4

Palatine, 55-6
Passat, 47, 95, 154
paying-off pendant, 119
Pelorus Jack, 145
Penelope, 28
phantoms, 53-75
Phoenix, 102
Pinta, 71-2
'piping the side', 120-1
Portland, 84
Poseidon, *see* Neptune

INDEX

punishments, 181-2
pursers, 172-3

QEII, 76
Queen Elizabeth, 50
Queen Mary, 24, 30, 50, 77, 119

R.E. Byrd, 103
'Rolling Home', 121-22
Rose, Sir Alec, 25, 26, 88
Royal Oak, 71
Royal Sovereign, 20
Rum, 105-6

sacrifices, 14-15, 30-1, 155-6
sails, 182-4
St Elmo's fire, 162-3
St Louis, 27
saints, 158-9
salutes, 118-121, 165
'Saturday night at sea', 106
'Savannah's Waving Girl', 75
sea-birds, 148-50, *148,* 161-2, *161*
seagods, 26, 30, 94, 110-18, *111,* 156-8, *157*
Seadragon, 23
seal, *141,* 146
seamen's goods, 90-1
sea-monsters, 125-38, *126, 127, 131*
sea-serpents, 125-38, *126, 127, 131*
shark, 143-4
ships'; badges, 23; bells, 36-8, *37,* 107-8; names, 23-8
ships; building, 13-28, *13;* burning, 44-5; company, 169-81; disposal, 50-52; ghosts, 53-75; in bottles, 82-4, *83;* jinxed, 23, 38-45; launching, 29-33, *31;* 'lucky', 45-6; Roman, 15-16; *see also* under individual entries
Sir Winston Churchill, 10, 34
Sirens, *137*
Slocum, Capt Joshua, 47, 71-2, 102-3
Spithead, 65-6
'splice the mainbrace', 105-6
Spray, 47, 71-2, 102-3
Sterling, 23
Strathdirk, 31
storms, 20, 95, 155-6

Superb, 26-7
'swallowing the anchor', 184

taboos, 14, 29, 76-99, 152-3
talismans, 76-88
Tartar, 83-4, *83*
tattooing, 80-2
Texas, 104
Thermopylae, 51
tides, 163-4
Titanic, 41-3
toasts, 106-7
Toye, Kenning & Spencer, 33
trade winds, 183-4
Tryon, Vice-Admiral Sir George, 67-9

U-boats, 10, 61, 64, 75
United States Coast Guard, 43, 54-5

Vanderdecken, Capt, 54, 58-61
Vanity, 140
Victoria, 67-9
Victory, 78, 112
'Viking funeral', 52
Violet, 64

Wahoo, 91, 114
Walker, Capt F.J., 71
Wales, Lieut the Prince of, 103, 124, 175
Warwick, 93-4
watches, 107-8, 173
waterspouts, 164
waves, 163
weather, 151-64
weddings, 105
West, Lieut-Cdr Frank, 145-6
whistling, 152-3
Whitfield, Capt George, 9, 43-4, 113, 145, 152, 166, 169, 170, 181
wind charms, 10, 151-6
winds, 182-4
witchcraft and evil eye, 14, *16,* 17, 78, 96-7
women at sea, 14, 20, 95-6, 155
wrecking, 55-6

Young Teazer, 57